I0477263

How To Scare The Hell Out Of Unemployment

Mike Bowman

DEDICATION

To my beautiful daughter Brooke, my greatest inspiration.

TABLE OF CONTENTS

Preface

Introduction

Summary: Unemployment is a serious threat to your short and long term financial well-being. It has the potential to leave deep economic scars in your household that may never completely heal. This book will show you many ways to rebound quickly from the swift, unexpected knockout blow that unemployment seeks to deliver.

Segments

Chapter 1

Standing Toe To Toe With Unemployment

Summary: This chapter discusses the practical and the psychological aspects of dealing with the initial start of unemployment. Organizing your financial and personal affairs is discussed, along with effectively managing your initial response to losing your job.

Segments

Chapter 2

Stop The Bleeding

Summary: Your savings, health, and the condition of your assets (such as a car or home) will erode without the money needed to spend on their preservation. Critical tasks you will have, while working to regain your employment, include taking preventative measures to minimize the financial risks you will face and safeguarding your current financial position.

Segments

Chapter 3

Unemployment Fighting Strategies

Summary: Unemployment does not have to be an economic death sentence. In this chapter you will find strategies to create opportunities to do better, maintain your standard of living, and even come back stronger than before.

Segments

Chapter 4

Investing In You & Your Things

Summary: You are your most valuable asset. In this chapter you will discover how to invest in yourself and how that investment pays you back in the various areas of your life.

Segments

Chapter 5

Finding Work

Summary: Fewer jobs and more competition means that getting a job offer today requires unconventional guerilla style tactics. You have to get in front of employers, stand out and quickly demonstrate value. This chapter shows you how.

Segments

Chapter 6 - Resources

Summary: This chapter will summarize many of the resources that will help you invest in yourself, prevent financial loss, maintain your quality of life, find work, and reduce expenses.

Some Of The Resources Listed Include:

Conclusion

Chapter References

Preface

My story

It was 6am and time to get up for school. It was a Wednesday, and I hated Wednesdays. Actually, every day had been bad during my first year at the new, small school my parents decided to send me and my two younger brothers to when I was 12. Wednesdays were particularly bad however, because we had gym class on those days. I hated gym class.

The school we were sent to was so small that all the boys in 7th through 12th grade were put together for gym. If you are not sure why that is a problem, think back to 7th grade. Kids can be brutal on each other sometimes! However, I had a few more disadvantages to contend with.

I was new to the school and I couldn't have stuck out more if I tried. A picture of me at 12 was a real life depiction of the stereotypical "geek". I was thin as a rail, wore giant glasses, had an awkward personality, tried to be funny with jokes that made absolutely no sense, wore the cheapest clothes Sears sold, and sported a buzz cut given to me at home in the name of both efficiency and cost control. To summarize, what that means to a 12 year old in gym class with 16 and 17 year old boys was I was a giant walking target.

Gym class

Bullying wasn't addressed as strongly back then as it is today. So when I was bullied in gym class I was mostly on my own to deal with it. The older boys took great fun in singling me out for abuse. There was the petty stuff like hiding my gym bag, locking me in or out of rooms, and tripping me as I walked around a corner.

Then there was the harder stuff like being hit. One time I was overheard saying I enjoyed watching wrestling on television. This inspired the older boys to demonstrate wrestling moves on me. I got beat up pretty bad. To be fair, several younger boys got this treatment, but I felt as if I got more of it.

Lunch time

Lunch time wasn't much better than gym class. Again, all the 12-17 year olds were together during lunch. You could try to stick with the boys closer to your own age, but there were plenty of days when trouble would just find you. One of the older boys' favorite lunch time antics was to inspect the contents of your lunch and determine if there was anything in it they would like.

It was generally accepted that fighting back would be a waste of your time, or worse, encourage harsher treatment. Another tactic the older boys had in their arsenal for keeping you in line was the threat of being embarrassed by them in front of other students. Being picked on was bad enough, but they seemed to have the power to put you in positions that were quite uncomfortable. You didn't just look like you were in a fight; you had pudding smeared up and down your shirt as well.

Turning point – the straw that broke my cupcake

One day at lunch I found a rare treat in my brown paper lunch bag. There were two chocolate cupcakes from Robert's Bakery. These were my favorite. A chocolate cupcake filled with whipped crème and topped with dark chocolate icing. I pulled them out of my lunch bag and set them in front of me, saving them for after the chipped ham sandwich. Then came trouble.

One of the older boys decided he was going to take one of my beloved chocolate cupcakes. I tried to stop him, but he got it away from me. I was furious. As ridiculous as it sounds now, the few minutes of enjoyment I would have received from eating that cupcake represented an oasis of escape from a day that would otherwise be bad. Now, this jerk was taking that away from me.

I lost it. Without thinking, I took the other cupcake and threw it at his face as hard as I could. The cupcake made a loud smacking sound when it hit the side of his face. The cake part fell off, but the chocolate icing was still stuck on his cheek. He looked both stunned and ridiculous with the round shaped icing smear hanging onto him. That wasn't the end of it though.

I jumped at his lunch, grabbed the whole bag and just started smashing it. Surprisingly, his friends didn't stop me, but found it rather entertaining. I didn't realize all eating had stopped in the lunch room and a teacher was sprinting toward me as I threw the older boy's crushed lunch at his face as well.

Aftermath

I received detention for my misbehavior and was required to apologize to the cupcake thief. I also had to eat lunch by myself for a few days at the table reserved for bad kids. However, despite the punishment I felt pretty good about myself. I had stuck up for myself, fought back, and in my mind had scored a small victory.

Another pleasant surprise was that there was no retaliation from the thief or older boys. In fact the amused comments from the cupcake thief's friends almost had a slight tinge of respect to them. Now there were far fewer problems in gym class and no one bothered with my lunchtime.

Lesson learned

Someone had tried to take something important from me, but when I placed my fear of retaliation and embarrassment aside, and fought back with intensity, not only did I prevail, but life was better for me afterwards.

What I couldn't have realized at the time was that gym class and lunchtime were relatively easy problems compared to the larger problems I would face as an adult. Unemployment was one of those problems.

Cupcakes and unemployment

It is a little embarrassing that it was my anger over a cupcake that taught me to stand up to a bully, but sometimes a real life story doesn't have movie-like glamour. To me, facing unemployment is not much different from facing the bullies at school. Many of the same attributes are involved. Fear, embarrassment, unfairness, and someone attempting to take something important away are all at play.

Randomness versus targeted

An extreme example of randomness happened in 1954. On November 30, 1954, Ann Hodges was napping in her Oak Grove, Alabama, home when an 8 ½ pound meteorite crashed through her roof, bounced off her radio after crushing it, and smacked her hard on her hip. There was no conceivable way Ann Hodges could have predicted she would be hit by a meteorite that afternoon. That was a completely random event.

Unemployment isn't just another random, spiritless phenomenon like a meteor shower, fire, or flood. Random means everyone has a near equal chance of being affected by the event. Ann Hodges' neighbor had just as much a chance of being hit as she did. Unemployment is much more predictable than it is random.

For one thing you can look at the health of the company you work for, the overall economic situation, and the industry you work in for indicators of potential employment trouble. Unemployment also tends to target those who are less educated, have fewer marketable work skills, have fewer resources or access to supportive services, or have insufficient work histories. In that sense, unemployment is like a bully with an agenda. It makes itself feel better by making the weak around it feel worse. That makes unemployment personal to me.

It has a mission to take your livelihood, systematically break you down financially and psychologically, force you into a mindset that believes you have no hope, and then leave your economic well-bring permanently crippled.

It knows that by embarrassing you with the stigma of being unemployed you may hunker down out of sight rather than putting yourself in the spotlight. It knows time is on its' side and that the longer you are unemployed the easier it is to wear you down financially. It knows it can use your fear of the unknown to paralyze your effort to find work by challenging you with employers who discriminate against the unemployed.

Unemployment thrives on those that aren't sure how to fight back, but, just like a bully, that is also unemployment's weakness.

The truth is most bullies are scared of being called out, and would much rather moves on to another victim, than face your challenge.

When you strategically fight and stand up to unemployment you are going to win. Sometimes when you are facing an unusually large and determined bully, like unemployment, it helps to have backup. I hope this book will be your back up, and show you how to scare the hell out of unemployment.

Mike Bowman

September 2011

Introduction

"We have nothing to fear, but fear itself." – Franklin Roosevelt

"Easier said then done" may be the fearful answer given by the millions of people who are facing or may face a loss of their income, and thus a serious threat against the standard of living they have become accustomed to. If you take a minute and think about what it means to have no income it would be easy to become afraid, but there is another choice: fight.

I've had to learn this lesson the hard way, as I have lost jobs more than once. There was a time when I was afraid of facing the world without the safety net of a steady job, but I am a fighter. Fear just wasn't an option, because fear wasn't going to feed my family. If fear is not an option for you anymore, you r only other choice is to fight.

This book will provide you many ways of defeating fear with knowledge, as well as, aggressively defending and promoting your personal economic security. We will closely examine unemployment, but the lessons apply to any situation where your income is threatened.

In the case of unemployment you know you will lose income. You know it will be a struggle to continue paying for health insurance. You know getting a loan, an apartment, or even another job, without a current job, will be extremely difficult. You don't know how you will pay your current bills, bills based on the income you used to make. You don't know how to find meaningful work, how your credit will be affected, how you will afford to get your car fixed, or how to deal with being torn from your work family.

This book will address those issues and will cover many topics such as the psychology of dealing with a job loss, preventing financial losses during a time of reduced or lost income, and quickly regaining meaningful employment.

We will also look at many ways you can maintain a standard of living very close to what you have grown accustomed to, and even emerging from this period of time financially stronger and smarter. You will discover ways to improve your education, the value of the things you own, and your own marketability in the work place. We will also talk about the numerous resources that are available, but not often advertised very well, that will accelerate your progress in quickly moving past this period of time.

Throughout this book you will see that it is planning and understanding, rather than fearing, that will allow you to successfully protect the financial well-being of you and your family. However, that is going to take focused, educated action on your part. One reason so many people are ill prepared for unemployment is that they have allowed themselves to fall into the freezing affect of fear.

Frozen by fear they curl up like hibernating bears and hope that they can just wake up after the economy has improved and carry on with their lives as if nothing happened. Unlike bears, though, we can not just sleep through harsh times. You are going to discover that while you should be concerned about losing income, you don't need to be afraid. When you are afraid it is easy to be paralyzed into inaction, thus making you a sitting target for economic deprivation. When you are concerned, you will take action to arm yourself with knowledge on how to protect, and even improve, your standard of living.

Jack's Story

It was late October 2008, and I was sitting in my office at work feeling sick. In my position at Roomful Express Furniture I was sometimes the person that told an employee their job was being terminated. I never liked doing that, but it was part of my job. However, I had never told someone that they were being laid off because the company couldn't afford their salary anymore. What made this day even harder was that I was instructed to have that conversation with Jack, who had been performing exceptionally well for me. I dreaded that meeting.

I would guess that Jack dreaded it more than I did though. He had done nothing wrong and with no prior notice was being asked to leave. Jack conducted himself professionally and with dignity throughout meeting, and even turned in several projects he had been working on before leaving the building. His behavior made me feel even worse about losing such an asset. Now that I was alone back in my office there were scary, and even selfish, thoughts crawling through my mind.

I felt awful for Jack. He was doing great and then without warning, what looked like a promising career at this company was ended. Even though he had been so stoic through the news, was he fully prepared for what was next? I felt guilty that I was relieved to still be employed. I knew I was unprepared for unemployment, and based on the news I was being told about the company's situation, I felt like my own salary resembled a giant bull's-eye on my back.

The next day.

I was convinced that things would not get better at work; that they would only get worse. Fear was running rampant through the company at this point, with everyone wondering who was next. At first I was afraid too, because I hadn't done much to prepare myself in the event I lost my job as well. How would I pay my bills or keep enjoying the quality of life I had become accustomed to? I made a conscious decision that day to not waste one more day on fearful inaction, but rather look at each additional day of employment as a gift and an opportunity to prepare for the worst.

There were two motivating factors that pushed me into action. The financial well-being of my family was the first. I had real trouble with the thought of them doing without or going through any kind of suffering because of my job loss. Secondly, I was disgusted by the fact that another person or place held that much direct influence over my financial situation, and that I had willingly placed myself in this position by becoming comfortable during the good years.

I certainly wasn't the first person to face this dilemma so I knew there were answers out there to all my questions. I just needed to look for them.

Storm Clouds On The Horizon

"Always plan ahead. It wasn't raining when Noah built the ark."
- Richard C. Cushing

Two more years passed at work and more rounds of layoffs occurred. Hourly and salary employees alike were let go. Morale kept getting lower. Negativity ruled as employees were required to do much more with much less. To a degree I became numb to the constant demands to cut costs, squeeze miracles out of air, and knowing my own job could be eliminated at any time.

I was not sure when my turn would come, but by the spring of 2010 I was ready. I was grateful for each paycheck I was still receiving, but if it would turn out to be the last one, I knew exactly what to do. For the last 18 months I had put myself through a college program of sorts. I had started my own business, learned new ways to protect myself financially, gained additional marketable job skills, and cut my living expenses without giving up my usual standard of living. These preparations would allow me to continue living the same lifestyle I was accustomed to if I lost my job.

My Turn

I had been laid off before and I knew how tough it could be when hit unexpectedly with losing your paycheck. In 2008 I knew it had the potential to be even worse as commerce and hiring had dramatically slowed throughout the country.

What got into him today?

My turn came 2 years after the job slashing had begun. The weeks before it happened I knew my time was up. Unfortunately, my experience at work during those last weeks was turning into the "about to be fired/laid off" stereotypes written about in the Yahoo Finance article "Signs You Are About To Be Fired".

The boss's typically rude and shunning behavior toward me suddenly become friendly and warm. Rather than arguing me into submitting to his misguided ideas, he would tell me I was right. His behavior and the overall climate in the company were too strange for me to just accept. I prepared for the bad news. It didn't take long until I was called to the boss's office for my lay-off notice.

Thankful.

After I received the news from the boss that my job had just been eliminated I went back to my office and thanked God. I am not an extremely religious person, but I acknowledged the fact that I had been given a head start and had gained a wealth of knowledge from very smart people that was about to start serving me and my family very well. It was time to start practicing what I had been studying and preaching.

The Quarter Roll.

"By failing to prepare, you are preparing to fail."
- Benjamin Franklin

The more I prepared myself for the financial storm I saw on the horizon, the more I realized how unprepared I would have been for unemployment. The same was true for many of my peers. It was no secret that the company was in trouble, but everyone reacted differently. Some of us started looking for work elsewhere, but at that time there were more companies laying workers off, rather than hiring, and we didn't come up with realistic options. While others believed the company would make it, I personally felt I didn't have a minute to spare in preparation.

The lackadaisical approach to the state of affairs at work was dangerous, and I decided to share the options I was finding with my peers anyway. I started a blog, which turned into a website, and then a magazine, which gave me a format to share the information I was finding about creating a less economically vulnerable household and career. That allowed me to form the foundation of a small business and communicate with others at the same time.

I named the magazine *The Quarter Roll* because it would be a publication about my conviction that everyone can do at least 25% better than they are right now. That means the information you need to earn more, pay less, get much more value for your money, and avoid financial loss is available to anyone. These 4 goals became the core principles of the business.

The business was born out of my desperate concern for security during insecure times. My theory was that if I could live on 75% of my earnings, but still enjoy 100% of the lifestyle I was accustomed to, the difference could be set aside and invested for the rainy days that were sure to come.

Ironically, the unbridled spending that defined the final years of Roomful Express Furniture also served as daily instruction to me regarding the destructive consequences of mismanaging your assets, budget, and income. Those issues also fell within the 4 core principles I was focusing on: learning new ways to earn more, paying less for living expenses, avoid financial loss by minimizing risks, and getting much more value for your money.

The writing on the wall.

"It's imperative we understand that every comfort zone becomes a "comfort trap" eventually." - Bill Phillips, Tranformation.com

Even if you are not laid off this book is for you. What millions of people learned over the last several years is that anyone can be threatened or hurt economically. The executive who told me I was losing my job was also instructed to leave the company, only 3 months later. In his case however, he had been there nearly 15 years. This executive felt fairly comfortable that his job was secure. However, like many more working people, he quickly realized it had been a mistake to relax into a comfort zone.

This book will talk about what to do when you lose your job, but will also serve as a primer for everyone else who wants to strengthen their immunity to the threats against their personal economic well-being.

Why Your "New Job" Is So Important.

"Success is dependent upon the glands - sweat glands." Zig Ziglar

You may receive a letter or some other type of document that states you are "unemployed" or a "dislocated worker", but you are far from jobless. The day you lose your job you are also starting a new job: quickly replacing your income. Ironically, this new job may look a lot like your old one.

For example, you are now in charge of generating income, meeting deadlines, finding ways to reduce costs, and negotiating better terms on existing arrangements. Make no mistake that this will most likely be the hardest job you ever had.

Sand just started collecting at the bottom of your economic hour glass.

Understand what is at stake. The minute your income is taken away, your "resources hour glass" is turned upside down, and the emergency funds, savings, and other assets you had stockpiled are now being drained away right in front of you. Your goal is to turn the hour glass back upright as quickly as possible and restock your resources. Let's discuss why.

"Economic scarring" is a term you should become very familiar with. If there is one point you get out of this book it should be this: your income directly determines your ability to provide a quality lifestyle for yourself and your loved ones. Any threat to your ability to earn a reasonable living is a threat against the enjoyment you and your family can expect to get out of life. The larger the decrease in your income is, the longer you can expect to experience a lower standard of living. In a sense your personal economic security is scarred.

Obtaining a new job will not necessarily bring everything back to normal. There is a strong possibility that if you are offered a job you will be paid substantially less than what you were previously making. In his article "Recession scars will linger long after economy heals", USA Today writer David Lynch says, "Millions of workers who've lost their hold on the labor market are seeing their incomes reset to a permanently lower level. Young people who entered the workforce this year can expect to earn substantially less during their careers than those who start work during booms."

Lynch continues, "Of those laid off, few will regain their previous standard of living. Even 15 or 20 years after being laid off, workers who lost their jobs during the recession of the early 1980s still earned a median 20% less than their counterparts who worked throughout the downturn, according to research by economists Till von Wachter, Jae Song and Joyce Manchester."

Any threat against your income or standard of living must be taken extremely seriously. It isn't just a matter of getting by for the next 3-18 months. There can be a tremendous strain on your saved resources as you work on getting by until you find a new job. As already mentioned, there is a good chance you will be offered equivalent work at much lower pay, possibly setting you back decades, financially speaking.

Your new task of finding work is a very important one. Look at the example given above. 20% was only the median (middle number) amount lost. Think about your old job for a minute. How long did it take you to increase your starting salary by 20%? Most likely you would like to avoid starting over that far behind from the salary you've become accustomed to. In order to avoid being economically scarred you must find equivalent work at equivalent pay at a minimum.

Working Like It Is The Day Before Vacation

"Its not knowing what to do, its doing what you know."
— Tony Robbins

Troy Polamalu's intensity.

On December 12, 2010 there was a vivid picture of intensity on the football field in Heinz Stadium in Pittsburgh. In the game's second quarter Troy Polamalu intercepted a pass by Carson Palmer. 45 yards away from the end zone Polamalu was determined to turn this opportunity into 6 points.

He fought for every one of those 45 yards, running like a hungry bear was chasing him. In those last 5 yards he brought together all of his intensity, experience, and training into superhuman like athleticism as he practically flew parallel to the ground into the very tip of the end zone to collect his 6 points.

There was still half a game to play. It wasn't like the Steelers desperately need the 6 points at that moment in the game, but that is how Polamalu plays. He plays like the team does desperately need those points, and more often than naught the team has been grateful to have those points in its' pocket when unexpected complications happen later in the game. That is why he is one of the league's most valuable players.

That is the same kind of intensity you must apply to earning more income and protecting your standard of living. The day your income is reduced or eliminated is the day your savings and unemployment benefits start to erode. Don't believe you are ok because you have 26+ weeks of unemployment insurance. Play to win right now; don't wait 26 weeks to attempt scoring a new job.

During this transitional time there is a lot on the line for you, economically speaking. In order to survive unemployment and come back stronger than before you are going to have to work harder and smarter than ever before. The intensity at which you will need to work will look like the typical day before a vacation. Knowing we will be leaving for vacation tomorrow, many of us will somehow be able to accomplish many times the normal amount of work.

On the day before vacation you are not a different person, but you are working differently. On that day you bring together all your influence, experience, and knowledge in order to immediately become more effective and accomplish much more work in a far shorter time. This book will help provide insights about getting back on your feet, and then it will be up to you to act on the knowledge you've gained and effectively turn your situation around.

Chapter 1

Dealing with a job loss

Chapter Overview

How many people will tell you that the people at work are like a second family? We say that because more often than naught we spend more time with co-workers than we do with our own families. Just like in a real family there are birthday and anniversary celebrations, meals together, projects together, and sometimes even trips together. Being asked to leave your job is a lot like being asked to leave your home. It hurts and you may not know what to do next.

The most unfortunate part of being asked to leave your second home is that your financial well-being was probably contingent on your paycheck. It is a double whammy: losing income and the most important social outlet you most likely had. In this chapter we will discuss strategies to answer the challenges this unique situation brings.

Reach Out, Don't Lash Out

"Control your emotion or it will control you." - Anonymous

Have you ever been in a car accident? There are car accidents you see coming and those that catch you completely by surprise. Being laid off from work is just like that as well. Sometimes the warning signs are all around you that trouble is imminent. Sometimes you don't see it coming.

If you are driving up a steep hill covered in winter ice and you see another car sliding down the hill sideways, you know you are about to get hit. You are not going to have enough time to react, but at least you saw it coming. However, the worst accidents are the ones that catch you completely off guard. You don't have time to inch over or brace yourself. One second everything is fine, the next second everything is chaotic.

Finding out you are being laid off may feel just like a car accident you were not expecting. All at once you are being forced to deal with extreme, out of the ordinary circumstances that could dramatically alter your life. All kinds of thoughts will rush through your mind at once. Your blood pressure may skyrocket, and the shock may take your breath away. It is important to remember that keeping your cool during traumatic events allows you to find more positive outcomes.

Meeting with your boss or human resources representative shouldn't be hostile or confrontational, but rather professional and calm. You didn't do anything wrong, and in most cases, company representatives are apologetic for the situation you are now facing.

You certainly shouldn't feel as if you have let anyone down or that you created this situation. In a meeting where you are being held accountable for a goal, project, or assignment you didn't complete properly you may feel the uneasiness of disciplinary pressure, but in this case it is the company that is failing, not you. Even so, very few people will feel comfortable during this conversation.

Why your comportment is important.

"Worry is the interest paid by those who borrow trouble." George Washington

People can act emotionally in highly stressful situations. Having your livelihood stripped away from you would certainly qualify as such an event. The feeling of losing control pushes some people into a panic driven state of mind. *That can only lead to negative consequences.*

There is a Bible story that dramatically illustrates the consequences of acting out in panic. Gideon was the leader of a greatly outnumbered army. However, using a clever trick in the middle of the night, he had his soldiers use clay pots, trumpets, and torches to create enough noise and confusion that the opposing army was convinced they were surrounded and outmatched.

In panic, the enemy army turned on each other in the darkness and confusion and killed each other resulting in a victory for Gideon. It was a tremendous lesson in the power of controlling your emotions.

A better way to invest your energy.

"I ain't got time to bleed"
— a wounded Blain from the movie Predator

I have had the great misfortune of both delivering and receiving job elimination news. When delivering the news, I tried to be as respectful, caring, helpful, and sympathetic as possible. However, there were many different reactions to the message I delivered. A few of the reactions I got stand out in my memory.

I had someone want to physically fight me. I had someone beg me to reconsider, even though it wasn't my decision. I had someone take the opportunity to tell me off. I had someone ask me if he could at least go back to his desk and bring me the assignments he had just completed as he knew I would need them for an upcoming project. (That one really got me.)

Don't get me wrong. It is ok to NOT be happy, but reacting in an extremely emotional manner during this meeting will not benefit you. You'll see why in just a moment. People can feel uncomfortable and awkward around someone who is crying or yelling uncontrollably. They may not know what to say or how to act so they recoil and find a way to quickly get away from the emotional person.

Someone who starts yelling or threatening is most likely going to be meeting with the police. Some people may want to run away from the news, literally. I had someone who didn't say a word and just got up and quickly exited the building. She didn't even stop to get her personal belongings from her desk!

When you react emotionally you are losing control of the rest of your time at work that day. The next 30-60 minutes are very important and you need to be composed. During the meeting with your boss or human resources department you will most likely cover issues like COBRA health benefits, your 401k, unemployment, and final pay. However, once the company has presented all this information to you, you have some important tasks to complete.

What to do with your time after a snake bite.

Dan Miller told an interesting story during his May 6, 2011 podcast about wasted energy on negative emotions. He said that when he was a kid he was out with a friend who got bit by a snake. Miller stated his gut reaction was to chase the snake with the intent of finding it and punishing it. His friend, however, sat down and cut the snake bite with a knife and sucked out the poison rather than chasing the snake.

What the snake did was wrong, but the reality was that the boy who had been bit would be far better off using his energy to remove the poison then hunting for the snake in order to get vengeance. The same is true when losing your job. When getting the news that you are losing your job you may want to lash out at the company, but at this point that will not get you anything. Your energy will be better spent on positive actions that will help put you in a better position to bounce back quicker.

Key Takeaway: Use the emotional energy you feel in a positive way. Don't waste a second on sorrow, revenge, or anger. Use that energy to create positive situations that will support your effort in quickly finding work.

You Aren't Going Anywhere Just Yet

"Ask, and it shall be given you; seek, and ye shall find."
– Matthew 7:7 King James Version

Before the meeting with your boss is over you should ask her for a commitment to a reference, another job in the same company, a part time job, a reduction in pay, or even a consulting job. There are many reasons to do this. Often in the frenzy of cutting payroll, the company sliced too deep. A week later the company realizes that there are vital functions not being completed and there is no one left to do them. It is not unheard of for a company to call back some workers a week later when they realize they can't live without someone in a particular function. If this happens, be sure you are on their minds since you proactively volunteered to come back or fill in at other jobs.

Also, ask your boss for a written reference. You are leaving the company only because of a downturn in business, not for productivity or disciplinary reasons, so your boss should be ok with writing the reference. That document will carry weight in future interviews.

Again, don't hesitate to offer to work in another department or location for the same company. Layoffs may be happening in your department, but the company may still have labor needs in other areas that you are not aware of. Your knowledge of company operations may be useful in other areas.

Asking for a reduction in pay, benefits, or hours is also an option that could be more attractive then unemployment. In most cases your unemployment benefit will come to about 60% of your regular pay. If you were allowed to continue working at a 20% reduction in pay or work 4 instead of 5 days you would still be further ahead financially. Of course, if you are given any of these options, don't relax. You were targeted once; nothing says it won't happen again next week.

Additionally, you should ask your boss to use her influence with the company's partners, customers, or vendors in finding you a job with them. Make the request before you leave. In the December 17, 2010 Pittsburgh Business Times article "Job seeker success stories: Four Pittsburgh-area workers share how they landed jobs", Brandy Mitchell mentions that it was contacting her old boss that led to her finding full-time work.

Your boss will more often be in a better position than you to know higher level decision makers in the industry or company that can assist you with finding new work. Just because this particular company is struggling doesn't mean the customers it serves, or the vendors and suppliers it purchases from, are also struggling. A personal phone call from your boss on your behalf, to another manager or influencer, can go a long way.

Be sure to visit this department before you go.

Be sure to stop by the Human Resources Department before the end of the day. One reason is to ask for the same things from the HR manager that you just asked from your boss. Ask for another job or a variation of your current job. If nothing is available, be sure to express your interest in applying your unique experience with the company in any other area as soon as the need arises. Be sure the manager has your current contact information.

Secondly, be sure to use this time to ask any questions you have about benefits, final pay, unemployment, various insurances through the company, and next steps. Staff members in the Human Resources department are a wealth of information and will be able to give you advice and information that will save you time and frustration.

Also, be sure to give the HR department a list of anything you may be leaving behind and will have to come back for later. An example may be office furniture or tools too heavy to take home that day. That will give you some assurance in keeping your personal belongings segregated and safe until you are able to return to pick them up.

Say good-bye to your work family.

Finally, be sure to say goodbye to your co-workers before you leave. If you don't say goodbye, you will definitely hurt their feelings. After all, we generally spend more waking time with our co-workers then our families. These people have become a pseudo family to you. Use this last opportunity to exchange current contact information if you haven't already. Staying in touch with these people will prove to be important in the weeks and months to come.

It is not uncommon to be asked to leave immediately. Some companies have explained this request as their attempt in minimizing what they feel will be a disruption caused by employees stopping their work in order to say goodbye. The company that would make such a demand from you after taking your job away isn't showing much respect for you, so why would you honor that request? Don't let that request stop you from saying good bye to your close friends. After all, they have been your second family.

Key Takeaway: Before you leave your job for the last time be sure to visit your friends and peers, because very soon you will be glad you did.

The First Thing You Should Do At Home

Your day still isn't over even after you have collected your things, talked to the boss and HR, said your goodbyes, called your significant other, and left work. It would be easy for anyone to get caught up in the whirlwind of the day's events and struggle to maintain their focus on what happens next.

The very first thing you should do when you get home is file for unemployment. This may sound like a no-brainer, but many people are arriving home that day shell shocked and feel the need to just sit still for awhile and let the news sink in. However, starting tomorrow morning, you most likely do not have another source of income. Your expenses are going to continue, and that makes getting your unemployment benefit as soon as possible very important.

When should I file for my unemployment benefits?

The sooner you file for unemployment compensation the sooner you will have income coming into your household. In Pennsylvania, for example, there is a waiting week. That means that there is no compensation to you during the week in which you first file your claim.

Remember, your "waiting week" is the week you file. In my own example, I was laid off on a Thursday. That evening, I filed online for my Pennsylvania unemployment benefits. Because I did this, my eligibility for benefits started on the 4th day after my lay-off, rather than the 11th day.

Even though it was Thursday night when I filed, that entire week was considered my waiting week. The following week was considered my first week of eligibility and I was paid compensation for the entire week. If I had chosen to wait until after the weekend, taking some more time to process the news I had just received, I would have been without income for an additional 7 days.

Why you must take ownership of this situation.

Your employer does not report to the unemployment compensation services that you have lost your job. They will confirm the facts of the event when asked by the state, but it is up to you to start the process. The first step in the process is filing the claim online or over the phone.

According the Pennsylvania Department of Labor and Industry "Initial applications for benefits may be filed online, 24 hours a day, 7 days a week at www.uc.pa.gov. Or, you may file by phone through a UC Service Center Sunday 9:00 a.m. to 4:30 p.m., and Monday through Friday 7:00 a.m. to 8:30 p.m."

Some people don't want to file immediately because they do not understand how unemployment benefits work and are afraid they may do something wrong if they act in haste. There are many resources available to walk someone through the process. The most immediate resource you have is the human resources department at work.

Most likely you are not the first person that has ever been laid off at your workplace and there have been people before you with similar questions. Your human resources administrator has worked with both the unemployment offices and the laid off employees, thus giving him a good understanding of how the process works. Be sure to tap into that knowledge.

Another reason someone may not want to immediately apply for unemployment is that they are taking a "head buried in the sand" approach. They just don't want to look this situation in the face and have to deal with it. They may be embarrassed they need the benefit, or feel that filing means failing. Unemployment insurance is just like any other insurance. You have been paying premiums on this insurance policy through automatic, state mandated deductions from your paycheck. If you were in a car accident you would file an insurance claim, just like you should do with unemployment. It is an insurance benefit you have paid for and are entitled to.

The reality is that every day that goes by and you don't file you are missing out on a day of income, and it is a serious issue that must be addressed right away. Your daily living expenses are going to continue. By filing immediately you can minimize the number of days you go without money coming into your household.

Key Takeaway: Don't delay addressing your unemployment insurance situation. The sooner you file, the better.

Now What?

By now it should be the day after the lay-off. You talked to your boss and the human resources department. You said good bye to your friends and co-workers and exchanged email addresses and phone numbers. You also filed for unemployment benefits last night before you went to bed, and printed out your application and any other confirmation pages and notes you were sent. Now, it's time to start talking about what happened.

The day after losing your job your head will probably still be spinning from the news, and it is easy for negative thoughts to creep into your mind. You may blame yourself for losing your job, worry about losing your money and assets, and what others may think of you now that you are unemployed. You will see that these thoughts are both a waste of your energy and more founded in fear than reality. Let's talk about refocusing your energy on positive actions you can take that will help you rebound much faster.

What did you do??

The unemployment office may tell you that you are a displaced worker. That means you lost your job through no fault of your own. So, again, when addressing the psychological aspect of losing your job, remember that there are millions of people just like you. You didn't do anything wrong! You are just a victim of the company's and / or country's economic circumstances.

The last several years have seen unemployment unlike that experienced in decades. These numbers give you a good perspective of how deep the recession was and an indication that healing will take more than a usual amount of time.

Unemployment rates 2007 – 2010

2007 – 4.6%

2008 – 5.8%

2009 – 9.3%

2010 – 9.6%

Source: Bureau of Labor Statistics

You may have lost your job for a number of reasons, but most likely they are all out of your control. In my own case it was a "perfect storm" of too much business debt and not enough cash flow at the company I was working for. Once the recession took hold, consumers stopped buying homes. Without home sales there was far less demand for new furniture, as people typically bought furniture during the process of moving. The company couldn't raise cash fast enough to keep up with the debt obligations and the business failed. That wasn't the employees' fault.

If you find yourself looking in the rearview mirror wondering what you did wrong, pull over for a minute. You didn't do anything wrong and you are not personally responsible for what happened. What you are personally responsible for is the well-being of your family. Look forward and begin rebuilding.

Should you be terrified of trying to live on half your paycheck?

I don't believe you should be terrified of anything, but any loss of income must be taken seriously. What is the first thing many people think of when they are laid off? Money. Where will money come from? How will one maintain their standard of living? What possessions, necessities, or conveniences will have to be given up for lack of enough money?

Money is like a drug to nearly all of us. Take away someone's drug and watch how they react. Take away someone's money and watch how they react. Money is a highly emotional subject because of the things we associate with money: kids' education, a car, a home, a vacation, or a gift for your spouse.

Too often we are also using money to fill a void in our lives. We mindlessly wonder the aisles placing trinkets into our carts that we feel will bring us some degree of happiness. The reason for the void is beyond the scope of this book, but the point is that it is not money you want; it is the things money gives you that you want. We are talking about having enough money to meet your needs (not wants). I'm convinced that you can do that on a lot less money than you thought you could.

You may have associated a sense of security to a particular amount of money, but what you will find out is that amount of money has actually lulled you into a misleading sense of comfort and wasn't a true representation of your actual economic need. That leads us to the task of honestly identifying what your actual financial needs are.

You are going to have to temporarily live on less money, but that doesn't automatically mean a lower standard of living. Can you get more for less? Yes, because you can learn to find and negotiate better deals, lower your costs, and squeeze much more value out of your purchases.

It is not unreasonable to be concerned about having your income cut. Remember though, you will receive an unemployment benefit so it isn't like you are going to be completely without income. You just have to be a little more resourceful, creative, and demanding when it comes to value. Once you've learned to wring $1.25 worth of value or more out of every dollar, the income pinch won't sting as bad while you pursue new work.

What does unemployment look like?

"Unemployment insurance is a pre-paid vacation for freeloaders."
California Governor Ronald Reagan, in the Sacramento Bee, April
28, 1966

Some people have been embarrassed to tell others that they are
unemployed. In one sense it is understandable. We grew up
seeing and hearing negative views about unemployment and
believed that the person who was unemployed was somehow at
fault. The unemployed person was seen as some kind of lazy
loser. He was a day time TV junkie who was leeching off of society
and expecting the rest of us to carry his weight. He was the
irresponsible guy who couldn't hold a job because he would sleep
in or fumble up the simplest tasks at work.

Of course, this image is far from the truth. You were standing at
your work station assembling widgets one minute and the next
minute you were in an office being told the company couldn't
afford you anymore. You may have been a model employee, but
the company wasn't going to be able to keep you. Don't allow the
thought to creep into your mind that you are somehow going to
be that sofa occupying, work hating non producer.

Today, there are millions of people just like you caught up in a
very tough economy, so we know that stereotype of old is
inaccurate. Don't hesitate to be open about your own situation.
Talking about it to others is part of refocusing on the task of
regaining the order you've had in your life.

One other important note to make is not falling into the trap of
making your job your identity. When someone starts to associate
their position or job title at their workplace with the way they

personally identify themselves it can crush their psyche when the job is taken away.

Don't confuse your identity with your role. Your role may be the Senior Person in the Big Company, but don't ever let that be your identity. The title of Senior Person was given by someone else. That person has the power to take away the title, and thus your identity, if you have associated one with the other.

A large part of your self-worth is gained by how you personally identify yourself. Never give someone else the power to take away your self-worth. I worked Jennifer Hull in the customer service industry for many years. During that time she had been promoted into a senior level position, which of course came with all the usual inclusions: pay, responsibility, and an important sounding job title.

What I will continually remember about Jennifer is that she was always able to keep things in perspective. One of the ways she did that was by separating her role at work from the way she personally viewed herself. What was Jennifer's daily reminder of what's important? She attached a custom plate to the front of her car. The plate didn't say "Very Important Senior Person at Big Company". It simply said "Christian's Mom".

Who you gonna call?

Here is why you wanted to be sure you had everyone's email address and their phone numbers. Talking about what happened is some of the best therapeutic medicine you can get for speeding up recovery from yesterday's shock. It is ok to email or text friends, but talking to them will be better. Hearing a friend's voice is much more reassuring. Most likely you are not the only one who lost their job yesterday. Call those people to express your support. Listen to their story and ideas and share yours.

This process will do several things for you personally. It is good for you psychologically. Human beings have a need to share and interact with others, especially during the most stressful times. Talking to others about what happened will help ease the stress associated with losing your job.

Talking to others may also lead to ideas on better ways to handle your situation. As you will see, there is a lot of work coming up that needs to be done in order to maintain your standard of living and regain your income. You may have some ideas on how to do that, but the best ideas come when many people are collaborating together and discussing various options.

How SEAL team members fight stress

Sean Silverthorne offered some good advice in his article, "How Navy SEALs Build Immunity To Stress", by mentioning this study: "George Everly, an associate professor of psychiatry at Johns Hopkins Bloomberg School of Public Health, has studied Navy SEALs and other groups that work under high stress. He said that people most likely to have developed an immunity to stress have a social support network, are optimistic, are persevering with a stout work ethic and value responsibility and integrity."

Reaching out and socializing with your friends and family will not only assist your job search, but also provide relief during a time of high stress.

Taking inventory.

"Scotty! What's left?" — James Kirk in Star Trek 2

In the 1990 movie *Star Trek II: The Wrath of Khan*, there is a scene where bad guy Khan steals a Federation starship and catches up with James Kirk on the Enterprise, another Federation starship. Much like a productive employee about to get unexpectedly smacked with a lay-off notice by an approaching supervisor, Kirk had a slightly uneasy feeling when he noticed this other starship slowly approaching, but didn't give it much concern. Why would he? It was a ship from his own fleet and everything appeared to be fairly normal. Sure enough, it wasn't.

Kirk and the Enterprise found out the hard way that there was nothing normal about that day. Once Khan got close enough he announced his intentions by shooting up the Enterprise. There was all kinds of chaos going on aboard the Enterprise as Kirk struggled to make sense of what was happening. Once the violence of the attack subsided, there was damage all around Kirk. The situation had changed dramatically in seconds.

You may be wondering what does this fictional event with the starship Enterprise have to do with being laid off. It is what Kirk said and did right after the attack that provides a great example of how you should act. Although shocked from the surprise attack Kirk kept his cool and immediately called down to Scotty the engineer and asked "What's left?". Kirk knew that, although he had just suffered a huge loss, his day was far from over. He wanted to take inventory of the assets he still had, and immediately get to work on reorganizing so that he could minimize any further damage.

Your approach should be the same. Realize that as devastating as this news was, you still have many tangible and intangible assets that you can call upon in order to regain focus and quickly get back on your feet.

Set two goals right now.

"Lose no time; be always employed in something useful."
— Benjamin Franklin

Once you have taken care of the basics of wrapping things up at work and arranging to collect your unemployment benefit, think about establishing a starting point from which you will be working. A great way to get started is setting two small goals for yourself. Setting these goals will get you moving and give you some direction during this time of transition.

Additionally, this will keep you focused on productive tasks during a time when you could easily slide into a non-productive, negative mindset brought on by abruptly losing the structure and schedule you were accustomed to. The saying "the Devil finds evil things for idle hands to do" applies.

Personally, I have seen the most positive outcomes come from people who set a physical goal and a psychological goal. Physical goals would include things like cleaning and organizing the entire house, detailing your car, painting a room, training for a 5k race, or winterize your home. It is a goal that 1) keeps you moving and out of a chair and 2) has an end result where you can physically see the fruits of your labor.

A psychological chore is one that challenges you mentally, and is exciting because it is something you really want to learn about or want to learn more about. Your goal may be learning to use a new software program, starting a blog, taking a college or non-credit adult learning course, or reading an entire series of books.

In both cases your goals have an end result that you can work toward. That will give you focus during a time that can keep you very unfocused. Ideally, your goals will support your efforts in regaining employment or enhancing your household income. Regardless if they do or not, you are putting some structure back into your life where structure was just taken away.

Walk it off.

"You can't just sit behind a desk all the time and think you know what is going on in the world. You have to go out and see it for yourself. You got to smell it. You got to taste it. You got to see it."
– Anderson Cooper

If you stop to dwell on any negative thoughts about your situation you are only robbing yourself of valuable time that could be used on regaining your income. We are going to talk about specific things you can do quickly to get a job or another income source, but there are supporting tasks you should be doing in order to keep your focus. The act of physically moving / working is a great way to stay in good spirits and keep yourself energized for the chores ahead.

Andy Defresne's story.

In the movie *The Shawshank Redemption*, Andy Defresne is a prisoner who was at the edge of a deep depression when he was faced with the reality of spending the rest of his life in conditions he found unbearable. While his best friend, Red, and fellow prisoners had given up on the thought of leaving, Andy made a choice to find a way out. It seemed like an impossible task, but eventually Andy did escape by tunneling out of his cell toward freedom. He didn't accomplish this all at once, but by taking one pocketful of dirt out of his cell each day and quietly dumping it outside, he eventually created a tunnel to freedom.

Andy achieved his goal by focusing on physically working on it a little bit every day. The extreme conditions he found himself in could have easily broken him psychologically, but the work he did with his hands kept him focused and saw him through that period of time. What can you physically work on that will support your efforts to meet your income goals?

Two ideas to get you moving.

First, take a part time job. In his book *Winning*, Jack Welch writes that employers are more willing to hire people who are already working. A part time job also eliminates gaps in your employment history, keeps you in a routine of going to work, and could give you up to date references.

Secondly, start exercising. When you are healthy you will look and feel more energetic. That energy will transfer over to your interaction with interviewers and help you stand out from other candidates. Most importantly exercise is a natural cure for the draining effect stressful situations can bring. In fact we will see in Tiki Barber's story that it was working out for an NFL comeback that broke him out of his depression.

Tiki Barber's story.

Tiki Barber was a NFL Pro Bowl level running back for the New York Giants. He had lived 10 excellent years in the National Football League when he decided to retire from the game.

In October 2006, Barber revealed his intention to retire at the end of the season. Even before that official announcement, Barber had been talking about retiring and starting a new career in broadcasting. When questioned why a player at the peak of his game would retire, Barber cited the toll the physical nature of football takes on a person's body. Once retired it didn't take long for Barber to get a job offer as a correspondent with NBC.

Barber had been enjoying three successful years in broadcasting until trouble arrived in 2010. Based on his acts of moral indiscretion with an NBC intern, NBC made the decision to cancel his broadcasting contract. Football was a deep part of Barber's life, so losing his full time connection to that world hit him particularly hard.

The Huffington Post probably said it best this way, "Barber said he was unable to deal with losing his $2 million per year job, which started as a football analyst for Football Night in America and progressed to a featured role on the Today Show. But his demotion to on-field duties and, eventually, to unemployment, led to depression."

Barber was quoted as saying, "I remember there were days where I would literally wake up, have coffee, get something to eat and sit on the couch and do nothing for 10 hours. I started to shrivel. I didn't have that confidence. I didn't have the, that aura anymore."

For an entire year Barber did nothing and his inactivity only fed his depression. It was only when many friends and coaches actively encouraged him to begin training again for a potential comeback into the NFL that Barber became physically active. By the summer of 2011 many news agencies were reporting on Barber's efforts to return to the NFL, a sign that he was actively working on making things happen for himself.

Depression is a real condition and it is often something you can't just talk yourself out of, as Tiki Barber discovered. For many people, losing their job is like losing their identity. A great deal of your self-worth and self-image is often tied into your work or career.

The Mayo Clinic says that when you are suffering from anxiety or depression, exercise is most likely the last thing you want to do. But once you get motivated, exercise can make a big difference. The Mayo clinic also suggest that exercise helps you gain confidence, take your mind off worries, get more social interaction, and cope with stress in a healthy way.

Key Takeaway: How you spend your time away from work is important to your physical and psychological health. Make positive choices that build you up rather than break you down.

Is That Opportunity Knocking At Your Door?

"When one door closes, another opens; but we often look so long and so regretfully upon the closed door that we do not see the one which has opened for us." Alexander Graham Bell

I was in a conference room sitting across from my boss at the long table. We were by ourselves and he had just delivered the proverbial "straw that broke the camel's back". With the negative atmosphere, layoffs, and stress I had been very negative and depressed about my job up to the point right before this meeting, but after the news I was about to receive it was actually about to get even worse.

Each day during the company's final months, I was either consumed with anger about what had become of my job, or I was planning on how to get out. I rationalized in my mind that acting on the idea of just walking out during a time when unemployment was so high was irresponsible and dangerous, but I just couldn't stop playing with the idea. Sometimes you reach the point of exacerbation where economic needs aren't the primary thing driving your thoughts anymore.

In the conference room, the boss took this surprise opportunity to tell me he wasn't fully pleased with parts of my performance. He had a prepared statement which he read to me; he said he chose to do it that way so he would convey his thoughts appropriately.

I listened in stunned silence as he noted items I had not accomplished; items the company had intentionally ensured, through the budgeting process, could not be completed. For example, all the incoming phone calls hadn't been answered. Even though I was able to mathematically demonstrate it was humanly impossible to answer all the phone calls with the current staffing levels I was also not allowed to spend money on overtime or hire new staff. In fact, I had been instructed by my boss to reduce payroll hours. It was a no win situation for me.

It wasn't so much the fact that the boss needed to make himself look better by telling the owner of the company he had scolded me for this "underachievement". It was how his intent was so nakedly displayed; he wanted to save himself during a time of layoffs by creating a situation to make me look less than competent. He had the power to do it, and he took the opportunity.

We had both turned into corporate pawns. Me for sitting there, putting more value on that job than walking out. Him for creating a "bad guy" in me, someone the company may now have a reason to justifiably layoff instead of him. That meeting immediately and dramatically changed our working relationship.

Months later when the boss told me I was one of many being laid off I didn't see my career ending, but rather an opportunity to move forward. Almost instantaneously I felt a sense of relief knowing that I now had a fresh start. Losing your job may appear like an end, but there is also a beginning. How many times during your career did you say you would have done things differently? How many times did you wish you had more education, time, or freedom?

The majority of us want out anyway.

The *Chicago Sun Times* reported in their January 5, 2011 article "84% of workers planning to look for new job: poll" that "Workers can't wait to dump their employers: 84 percent of respondents to a survey say they plan to actively look for a new job this year. That's up from 60 percent who said they planned to do so last year. Only 5 percent said they intend to stay in their current position." Look at this situation's positive side. Even if you loved your job, you may have been able to accomplish more, earn more, or enjoy more if you had the chance to do things differently up front.

One door may have closed for you, but that means another one is opening. What do you want to accomplish? Do you want to learn or update your work skills, or even work in a different industry? Do you want to strengthen your personal economic security? Would you like to stop worrying about being financially vulnerable and become strong enough to weather the toughest economic storms? Let's get to work on making it happen.

Key Takeaway: What do you really want to do? This could be the opportunity you've been waiting for.

Chapter 2

Stop The Bleeding

Chapter Overview

Unemployment can be like a stab wound. It is stuck deep into your personal financial situation and your assets are going to start bleeding. In this chapter we will discuss preventing financial loss and minimizing your risks while facing a reduced income. The first step is to stop the financial bleeding. The second step is to use strategies that serve as armor that will protect you from further injury.

Your Credit Rating

A bank is a place that will lend you money if you can prove that you don't need it. Bob Hope

Your credit rating may be one of your most important allies during a time of unemployment. It is someone who will vouch for you and tell others that you deserve help. Credit ratings are used by many different entities such as landlords, utility companies, banks, insurance companies, professional licensing organizations, credit companies, and sometimes employers. That means it is important to you as a job seeker, as someone who want to reduce expenses, and someone who may need a helping hand with financial matters.

Because your credit rating is so important you need to pay special attention to taking any necessary steps in preserving a good record. Of course the challenges of being unemployed may put you at risk of falling behind on payments. Protecting your credit rating should be a priority. It is not only important to your situation now, but future challenges you may face. Remember your credit report keeps long term accounts of your financial behavior.

The very first step is free.

Start by ordering your free annual copy of your credit report. You can do that through annualcreditreport.com. Review your report and be sure that you take the appropriate steps in correcting mistakes.

Already got your free report this year? As an unemployed person you are entitled to a second free report per the 2003 Fair and Accurate Credit Transaction Act (FACTA). You may need to call each of the 3 major credit report bureaus on your own, tell them you are unemployed, will be looking for work within the next 60 days, and would like a free copy of your report.

3 important reasons to care about your credit rating.

This is an excerpt from the December 2010 issue of *The Quarter Roll*:

1. A good credit rating means you will pay less to borrow money.

Even with the best intentions, budgeting, and expense control, you may need to borrow money at some time in your life. For example, purchasing a house will typically require some amount of borrowing for most people. The interest rate you pay on a home loan will make a dramatic difference in the total amount you pay over time. Your credit rating will determine what rate you are offered.

Example: a 30 year, fixed rate loan of $50,000.00

-At 7%: $332.00 monthly payment and a total of $69,754.45 interest paid

-At 5%: $268.00 monthly payment and a total of $46,627.89 interest paid

2. A good credit rating is becoming your character reference.

The days of having your minister, boss, local sheriff, and even your mom vouch for your character are gone. Today, we need to accept that, in more cases then naught, our creditworthiness is judged by our credit score numbers.

Keep in mind that your credit history and score can affect rates you are quoted by utility and phone companies, for example, as well as your ability to rent an apartment.

3. A good credit rating is like a safety net during economic hardship.

You may comfortably live on a cash basis, but the reality is that economic hardship can hit anyone today. Many people are faced with circumstances they never thought they would have to deal with. In the event you need to borrow money on a short term basis during a personal hardship, having an excellent credit rating could be the safety net you need in order to get access to cheap money for a short period of time.

What will and will not affect your credit score.

With the amount of emphasis put on credit you may start to wonder if being unemployed may have some impact on your rating. Credit is not affected by job loss. It is based on your payment history and the other factors listed below. You do not need to call the credit card company and tell them you are unemployed.

Understand how your credit rating is determined.

A clear understanding of what will and will not affect your credit rating will allow you to organize your finances and maintain a good report.

myFico.com is a good resource to learn more about credit reports. Here are the things that will affect your credit rating as listed on myFICO.com:

Payment History – 35% of your score

-Account payment information on specific types of accounts
(credit cards, retail accounts, installment loans, etc.)

-Presence of adverse public records (bankruptcy, judgments, suits, liens, wage attachments, etc.), collection items, and/or delinquency (past due items)

-Severity of delinquency (how long past due)

-Amount past due on delinquent accounts or collection items

-Time since past due items (delinquency), adverse public records (if any), or collection items (if any)

-Number of past due items on file

-Number of accounts paid as agreed

Amounts Owed – 30% of your credit score

-Amount owing on accounts

-Amount owing on specific types of accounts

-Lack of a specific type of balance, in some cases

-Number of accounts with balances

-Proportion of credit lines used (proportion of balances to total credit limits on certain types of revolving accounts)

-Proportion of installment loan amounts still owing (proportion of balance to original loan amount on certain types of installment loans)

Length of Credit History – 15% of your credit score

-Time since accounts opened

-Time since accounts opened, by specific type of account

-Time since account activity

New Credit – 10% of your credit score

-Number of recently opened accounts, and proportion of accounts that are recently opened, by type of account

-Number of recent credit inquiries

-Time since recent account opening(s), by type of account

-Time since credit inquiry(s)

Types of Credit Used – 10% of your credit score

Number of (presence, prevalence, and recent information on) various types of accounts (credit cards, retail accounts, installment loans, mortgage, consumer finance accounts, etc.)

Here are examples of things that will not affect your score:

-You were fired, laid off, or are now collecting unemployment.

-You are going back to school and paying with cash, a grant, or a scholarship.

-You took an early withdrawal from your 401k plan and paid a penalty.

-Your occupation has changed.

Key Takeaway: Today, your credit rating is literally your reputation, and could very well be a determining factor in getting a new job. Take the appropriate steps to safeguard it and enhance it.

Scammers Who Prey On The Unemployed

"If it seems too good to be true, it probably is." Gary Adler

There are enough influences in our world trying to take advantage of us that it can make your head spin sometimes. Have you ever heard that human beings do not have any natural predators? That can not be an accurate statement. There may not be any animals intentionally looking to eat us, but we are being hunted. Scammers prey on us every day. These scamming predators are very resourceful, and when they see an opportunity to attack they swoop in quickly.

These past several years have been prime job scamming years. People's desperation or hardships is what makes them most vulnerable to scam attacks, and the economy has produced many such people. Many people are searching for work and instead are being scammed out of their personal information. What was supposed to be a job search turned into identity theft.

Job scammers first lay a trap. They advertise an open position with their "company" or in a well-known company. They may solicit you directly. Their intent is to lure you into applying for work and in the process steal your identity. When you apply for the job you are asked for information that can be used to rob you. Many victims have found that after supplying the "interviewer" with their personal information they never hear from the "company" again. Instead they find out that their identity has been used for fraudulent activity.

How do you protect yourself from this scam? First, thoroughly check out the company you are applying to. This exercise should be part of any pre-interview work anyway so that you can intelligently talk about the company during an interview.

Legitimate companies that intend to hire you may do a background check on you, so why not do one on them? You may want to purchase a background check on the company and look for liens or lawsuits that indicate trouble. What can you find out about them on the web or in the news? Look them up on the Better Business Bureau website. View their facility using Google Earth. Visit the company prior to interviewing and look for signs of legitimate business being conducted.

Secondly, do not give out sensitive information until a job offer is imminent. A paper or digital application being handed to a nameless cashier or receptionist or a lifeless computer server is no place to give your sensitive identification information.

Be careful to protect things like your social security number, picture, professional license number, and driver's license number. Once you have gone through enough of the interview process to feel comfortable with the company, you can provide the information they need to check references or your background.

More tips to avoid scams.

=Never give personal bank account, PayPal or credit card numbers to an employer.

=Do not transfer money and retain a portion of the payment.

=Never forward, transfer or "wire" money to an employer.

=Do not re-ship products or partake in cross-border action.

Scam warning signs.

=Interviews are conducted in a hotel room, living room, office in vacant building.

=You are asked for sensitive information prior to an interview.

=You are asked for your banking information, a registration fee, or enrollment fee.

=There is no pay during training.

=You have to buy tools, merchandise, or other items directly from the employer.

=You will be charged for company controlled equipment.

=The "employer" wants to scan your personal identification instead of making a paper copy for the IRS.

=The company does not answer the phone when you call. It either continues to ring, is answered by voice mail, or answered by someone who sounds suspiciously clueless.

=The job sounds too good to be true. Some of the fake 2010 BP oil spill ads falsely promised large salaries and to pay for all living expenses while residing in the beach areas of the Gulf.

CareerBuilder.com also offers these additional warning signs:

=A contact e-mail address that is not a primary domain. Jimmyjoe@yahoo.com versus jimmyoe@jimmyjoesgarage.com.

=Misspellings and grammatical mistakes in the job ad.

=A lack of interest in meeting you in person.

Spending Money Emotionally

Many people in my life are smokers. Considering all of the health risks smoking brings, I often wondered why someone would even start this habit. Perhaps it is because they seem more relaxed when smoking. I noticed that when they do their taxes, try to find an address in a new neighborhood, or hurry to put together a bicycle before Christmas morning, they would smoke to relieve their stress.

The smokers in my life smoke when they need something to calm them down. The stresses they face challenge them emotionally and the smoking helps alleviate that stress. All of us face emotionally draining challenges, such as unemployment, and may start looking for something that provides some relief. Smoking is just one bad habit that brings temporary repose, but it comes with so many unwanted side effects. Spending money is another bad habit.

Why does spending money feel so good?

The 2010 film *Inside Job* is an Oscar-winning documentary about the deep-rooted corruption that led to the global economic meltdown of 2008. Andrew Lo, Professor and Director of the MIT Laboratory for Financial Engineering, is interviewed in this film.

He stated, "Recently neuroscientists have done experiments where they've taken individuals and put them into an MRI machine, and they have them play a game where the prize is money. And they noticed that when the subjects earn money the part of the brain that gets stimulated is the same part that cocaine stimulates."

Buying things can temporarily make you feel good. Here is an article from *The Quarter Roll* magazine that proposed spending money is one of the most addictive behaviors we do.

4 reasons why spending money may be the most addictive behavior.

1) Spending money is ruthlessly marketed to you.

You are overtly encouraged via advertising to spend your money on thousands of different things. Spending is covertly encouraged, for example, by product placement in TV shows. It is inferred that you will be better off if you look, live, travel, sleep, or even smell like highly compensated celebrities.

2) Spending money is extremely easy.

You can shop online or at a store, use store or major credit cards, take out a loan, have automatic deductions from income checks, get advances on tax refunds, use payday loans, put merchandise on layaway, get short term "same as cash" financing, use gift cards, and even use old fashion cash! There are endless easy ways to spend money.

3) Spending money is rewarded with recognition.

Who will receive more positive attention today? The woman who saved $200.00 by purchasing new work clothes at the Goodwill, or the woman who spent $200.00 on a stylish new dress at the boutique? The guy who paid cash for his "new" 10 year old car, or the guy who leased a new luxury sports car? The guy who packed his own lunch or the girl who is wearing new diamond earrings? The guy who gave $100.00 to charity, or the guy who just bought everyone another round? The positive attention we are rewarded with when spending money validates the behavior in our minds.

4) Spending money is the patriotic thing to do.

A famous President George Bush quote came late in 2006, when worries of a recession were taking hold, and the advice we received from him was to "go shopping". Today, even as we still recover from the Great Recession our government leaders encourage us to spend in order to allow the creation of more jobs. The nation hovers around the consumer confidence index in hopes we are spending more.

When you have lost your job it is natural to feel insecure, scared, and even depressed. You may be tempted to find something that will help alleviate these negative feelings. You certainly wouldn't consider drugs or other immoral and illegal activities so perhaps you think about spending money on yourself for a quick pick me up. The problem is that filling the void with money can quickly push you from a bad financial position to a financial wreck.

Find a positive way of dealing with your stress. Some people will start a blog to talk about their job hunting activities and to share ideas. Work on home projects, learn a new skill, make a new friend, or maybe even write a book!

Saving Money Emotionally

In one early scene from the movie *Taking Woodstock*, the main character Elliot Tiber is at the bank with his mother Sonia begging the bank manager for more time to pay the mortgage on the family's business and home, The El Monaco Motel. Sonia insists she has no money and that the bank should be ashamed of itself for wanting to foreclose on a Russian immigrant struggling to make a living.

In another scene, much later in the movie, it is revealed that Sonia had been hoarding money, when Elliot finds her sleeping on a large stack of cash. In fact it was $97,000.00 hidden under the floorboards of her bedroom closet. Sonia had grown up extremely poor and was in constant fear of there not being enough money. This led her to feel compelled to hoard money. That fear led her to forego the responsibilities of paying bills in favor of keeping the cash within arm's reach, even knowing that could mean losing her business and home. Having the cash nearby gave her a feeling of security.

Some people who lose their jobs may feel the same way as Sonia did. They may have developed an emotional relationship with money because of the things they acquaint with it. They may decide that they will forego paying their bills and rather save every dollar because they are afraid of further financial losses, which in turn means a loss of their way of life or security.

In this case, the problem is that saving money can actually detract from your quality of life. If you do not keep up on your financial obligations you will start a domino like effect that can ruin your credit rating, as well as, put your home and other assets at risk.

Of course it is good to save money. In fact it is wise to spend much less on non-essential items. However, putting your home, car, good credit, and other assets at stake for the purpose of building a cash cushion may very well have the opposite result you were looking for.

Creating an emergency fund is a fantastic idea, but that should happen before you lose your job, not after. If you don't have an emergency fund and you have lost your job, your focus should be on finding ways to replace your lost income and preserving the assets you already have. Taking the rent money, putting it into a savings account, and then being evicted from your apartment makes no sense. Now is not the time to think about saving for retirement, dream vacations, or college. It is a time to preserve the things you do have and then find new income options.

Spending Money For Convenience

One of the "problems" of having a steady job is that it is easy to justify convenience purchases. The second problem is that when the steady job is gone we are so accustomed to living with the conveniences that it hurts all most too much to give them up.

Mandy's story.

Mandy had a great job. She was a professional working for a large corporation and made a terrific salary. The tradeoff for this great job was that she worked 55-60 hours a week and had a one hour commute both ways. What she had in income she gave up in free time. Time was always a concern for Mandy. In order to facilitate her long work hours she spent a good deal of money on convenience items.

Mandy bought prepared breakfasts and lunches when working. She had someone clean her house, do her laundry and ironing, shovel snow, pick up her car for repairs, walk her dogs, wash her car at work, and run errands. Unfortunately, Mandy lost her job due to the recession. She had grown accustomed to having access to convenience related services, but soon realized convenience costs substantially more than doing it on your own!

You may not have had someone coming to your job to wash your car, but what convenience items are still in your life and costing you extra? Are you paying extra for the convenience of making payments on something? Are there fees for paying your bills online or over the phone? Are you buying movie tickets online? What can you do for yourself and avoid paying for the service all together?

Key Takeaway: We all do weird things with money on occasion, but right now is not the time to be irresponsible with your money. Identify what your weaknesses are when it comes to managing your money, and take the appropriate action necessary to address them.

Chapter 3

Maintaining and Thriving

Chapter Overview

Any length of time away from work means less money coming in to your household. In this chapter we will focus on maintaining your standard of living by finding better values and alternatives, reducing costs, and generating part-time income.

As a displaced worker your primary income will most likely come from unemployment compensation, but as you will see, the radical changes in unemployment laws and total benefits have not been fully understood by many people. Understanding how the system works will allow you to strategically manage your resources.

During this time you will focus on preserving and maintaining things such as your work skills, assets, health, credit rating, and your family's routine. Yes, you may need to get used to alternatives that will facilitate preserving your financial position and job search, but after exploring these alternatives you may wonder why you never used them before.

Class in session: Unemployment 101

Earlier we discussed the importance of filing for your unemployment compensation benefit. Unemployment insurance is like other kinds of insurance in the sense that you pay a regular premium, deducted out of your paycheck, and are provided with monetary compensation in the event of a loss; in this case that means losing your job.

Payment into the state unemployment program is required by law; it is not optional. However, you are not required to file a claim for unemployment if you don't want to. Regardless of your intent to file an unemployment claim, it is a benefit you are entitled to.

The amount of compensation you can expect to receive depends on many factors, including how long you have been working and how much you earned during that time.

Unemployment compensation benefits traditionally last up to 26 weeks in most states, and they are managed by your state government. In 2008, as millions of people lost their jobs, it became evident that any new hiring was also dramatically slowing down. This created an unusual situation where more people were still looking for work even after exhausting their full slate of state unemployment benefits.

With millions of workers still actively searching for a job, the federal government also agreed to provide unemployment benefits to those who had exhausted their state compensation.

These federal unemployment benefits are called Emergency Unemployment Compensation (EUC) and are distributed in tiers.

How do the unemployment tiers work?

With unemployment rising quickly in 2008 then President George Bush signed a bill to approve the extension of federal unemployment compensation. That meant that the federal government would continue to provide money to dislocated workers who had exhausted their state benefits.

The federal government breaks down levels of assistance into "tiers". We started hearing about the "99ers"; people would qualify for 99 weeks of compensation. Many people wrongly assumed that anyone who was unemployed would receive 99 weeks of benefits. There are three important things to know about federal unemployment tiers and extended benefits.

The four unemployment tiers.

The first thing you want to understand is the number of tiers and the number of weeks assigned to each tier. As of this writing in late mid-2011 there were 4 tiers that are scheduled to be in effect, based on your state's unemployment rate, until January 3, 2012. Here are the numbers of weeks assigned to each Emergency Unemployment Tier:

EUC Tier I is for up to 20 additional weeks if you have exhausted regular UC benefits. This level is contingent on the phase out deadlines.

EUC Tier II is for up to 14 additional weeks and is contingent only on the phase out deadlines.

EUC Tier III is for up to 13 additional weeks if your state's previous 3 month average is 6% or higher.

EUC Tier IV is for up to 6 additional weeks if your state's previous 3 month average is 8.5% or higher.

This means that if you have exhausted your 26 weeks of state unemployment benefits, you are eligible to begin Tier 1 of EUC, which would provide you up to 20 more additional weeks of compensation.

The second important factor is your own state's unemployment rate. The reason you keep seeing the words "up to" is because these additional weeks of compensation are contingent on your state's unemployment rate, not just the country's unemployment rate. You will be eligible for fewer tiers as your state's unemployment rate falls. Key milestones are at or above 8.5%, 6%-8.4%, and below 6%.

For example, tiers will begin to phase out in your state as the unemployment rate falls to 8.4% and then 5.9%. For example, Pennsylvania announced on March 14, that the three month average unemployment rate had fallen to 8.4%, thus the 6 weeks of Tier 4 benefits were being eliminated as of April 2, 2011.

How to extend the number of weeks you get unemployment compensation.

There is another caveat to how long you can collect unemployment benefits. At each tier of unemployment you are assigned a maximum dollar benefit. How is that amount determined? In Pennsylvania, for example, the Department of Labor and Industry says, "Your financial eligibility is based on the wages you were paid and the credit weeks you earned during your base year (base year: the first four of the last five completed calendar quarters prior to filing your claim)."

Say your total financial benefit for one tier of compensation is determined to be $10,400.00. If you are in Tier 2 that amount will be divided by 14 weeks and give you a weekly payment of $400.00 per week.

What is a partial benefit credit?

You will also have the opportunity to earn a partial benefit credit. That means you can earn up to a certain amount, perhaps you found a part-time job, without your weekly benefit being reduced.

As an example, your determination letter may say you are on Tier 2, will be paid $400.00 per week, and can earn up to $150.00 per week from a job, without any money being taken away from your $400.00 benefit. Thus, you take home $550.00 that week; $400.00 from unemployment compensation and $150.00 from your part-time job.

A bad argument to make.

Some people will argue they don't want to earn more than $150.00 a week, and may even refuse a job that pays $200.00 per week, because they feel they are losing unemployment compensation benefits. This is short sighted. Here's why.

Let's say Ben fits into the scenario we have been using. He is being paid $400.00 per week from unemployment. He finds a part-time job that pays $200.00 a week; $50.00 more than his partial benefit credit. Now he will be paid $350.00 from unemployment, as $50.00 will be deducted from his original weekly benefit. He will still bring home $550.00 per week, but now $350.00 comes from unemployment and $200.00 from his part-time employer. Does Ben just lose that $50.00 he gave up from unemployment? No.

How Ben extends his unemployment benefit even further.

Ben is in Tier 2, qualified for a total benefit of $10,400.00, and was going to receive $400.00 per week until he got the part-time job that was paying him $200.00. Because he isn't using $50.00 of his benefit each week it is saved for additional weeks. If Ben didn't use $50.00 of his benefit for the 14 weeks he is on Tier 2 he still has $700.00 left at the end of 14 weeks ($50.00 x 14 = $700.00).

In this case Ben does not need to file for Tier 3 benefits just yet. For him Tier 2 will actually be 16 weeks instead of 14 because he still has $700.00 left over. Ben will still collect $350.00 per week for the additional two weeks ($700.00 / 2) and will have extended the length of time he is receiving unemployment benefits.

Extended unemployment benefits.

Thirdly, note that federal emergency unemployment benefits (EUC) are paid before state extended benefits (EB) are paid. EUC is a federal initiative. EB is a state initiative. If you have been unemployed long enough to exhaust your initial state benefits and then the various federal tiers of EUC, you may qualify for extended benefits through your state.

The Pennsylvania Department of Labor and Industry explained it this way in February 2011, "The Pennsylvania UC Law was recently amended to increase the maximum amount of EB a claimant may receive if Pennsylvania enters a 'high unemployment period,' or HUP. A HUP occurs when

Pennsylvania's total unemployment rate reaches 8 percent. Pennsylvania's total unemployment rate has risen to the level necessary to create a HUP."

"As a result of the HUP, if you were financially eligible for 13 weeks of regular EB, your financial eligibility is increased to 20 weeks. If you were financially eligible for 8 weeks of regular EB, your financial eligibility is increased to 12.8 weeks."

What happens if you have exhausted your federal unemployment tiers?

In Pennsylvania, for example, if you've gone through all the tiers of federal unemployment compensation and the average unemployment in the state for the last three months has been 8% or higher, you will qualify for 20 more weeks of benefits, at the same monetary amount you have been receiving. If the three month average was 6.5% to 7.9% you would receive 13 weeks. These benefits are paid from the state.

Not all states are perfectly clear about what you should do when you have exhausted one tier of unemployment benefits. This is why it is important for you to personally track what week you are on and where you fall within the benefit tiers. Here is why you should file a new claim for emergency benefits the very day you exhaust regular benefits.

Angie and Todd were both laid off at the same time in Pennsylvania. They both qualified for 26 initial weeks of unemployment, and both filed claims online every other Sunday. Neither found a job within 26 weeks. At the 26 week mark they both discovered, while filing online as usual, they were out of regular benefits; no further information was given.

Todd knew he would qualify for EUC so he decided to wait for further instruction on what to do. Angie, on the other hand, called her unemployment office immediately as their call center was open on Sundays. The representative filed a new claim for Angie over the phone. Angie received a direct deposit within 7 days.

Todd received a letter from the unemployment office 5 days after he discovered he had exhausted regular benefits. The letter gave instructions on filing a new claim. The next morning Todd filed a claim for EUC via the mail and received his direct deposit 15 days after that original Sunday. Because he waited to act, Todd was forced to wait an additional amount of time for his payment.

Hopefully, you will not find yourself in a position where you have gone without work for this length of time. If you do, it is important to understand how your compensation may be affected by laws enacted or retracted by Congress, your state's unemployment rate, and your state's laws in regard to extended benefits. Remember, that some states may not automatically notify you that you are eligible for the next tier of benefits. Again, it is up to you to closely monitor what week you are on and then call your unemployment office if you have not received instructions to refile or renew your claim.

Key Takeaway: The rules for unemployment compensation have changed and will most likely change again. Keep track of what week and tier you are in and quickly follow up with the unemployment office when changes occur.

Crunching Numbers Into Dollars

Roseanne was a senior assistant manager at Eat'n'Park restaurant during the 1990s. If anyone needed a face for a cost control poster she would have been the person to portray. When

Roseanne was on duty the staff knew that the dishwasher would not be run with only one rack of dishes in it, extra condiments were given by request only, and you didn't eat a French fry you didn't pay for. The worst sin, however, was being caught still walking to the time clock in order to punch out 30 seconds after your shift was scheduled to end.

That restaurant was often commended for the ability to stay within budget. Most of the kids working there didn't fully understand what that meant, but it's a good bet that Roseanne could have taught a graduate level class in cost control.

The restaurant did give Roseanne a chair to sit on while completing paperwork, but she was never seen sitting. Rather, it seemed one of her favorite things to do was visit every inch of the restaurant and record notes of inefficiency with the clipboard and pencil that rarely left her hand. Perhaps her second favorite thing to do was show you how YOU could be more efficient!

Just like Roseanne insisted that every last drop of ketchup be squeezed out of a bottle before it was thrown away, you must learn to squeeze every last penny of value from a dollar. It is no longer acceptable to get 100 pennies for one dollar. Now, you must insist on getting 125 or more pennies for every dollar.

Part of your strategy needs to be strategically reducing your costs. That means continuing to get the things you need, but for much less money. It can also mean paying the same amount, but receiving much more, thus extending an item's useful time between purchases and reducing your overall cost per unit. This is a great way of supporting the standard of living you are used to, but on a lower income. Roseanne had no problem with putting a cherry on top of a milkshake, but you would never see two, unless you bought another milkshake!

A great way to start is by following Roseanne's example. Get a notepad and pencil and start visiting every corner of your home. Just start taking notes. Is there a faucet leaking or toilet running non-stop? Is there cold air coming through a crack around a window? When was the last time you cleaned the refrigerator coils? Do the kids leave the garage door open? Are you tires properly inflated? Are you buying more food than the family is eating? Are you insuring a motorcycle you never ride and would rather sell? Take lots of notes. Nothing is too trivial right now. You may not act on all these observations, but it will give you lots of information that will help you identify areas of waste that are needlessly costing you money.

Credit cards and debt payments.

Do you use a credit card? Are there balances due on your credit cards? If you answered yes, you are not alone. Citing a U.S. Census Bureau report, Money-Zine.com wrote, "In 2010, the US census bureau is reporting that U.S. citizens have over $886 billion in credit card debt and that figure is expected to rise to $1.177 trillion in 2011. More specifically, the report states that each card holder has an average credit card debt of $5,100.00 and this number is projected to reach $6,500.00 by the end of 2011."

If you are unemployed and still receiving credit card bills in the mail, you are probably wishing you wouldn't have spent that money in the first place. Since you can't go back in time and get that money back let's focus on what to do now.

Your first step will be to take strategic steps in reducing your overall credit debt and monthly payment obligation. You can do that by calling your credit card holders, explain your situation, and ask for a more workable payment plan. Simply defaulting on the payments is an option of absolute last resort. If you stop making payments or start to pay late you are going to start damaging your credit rating.

Remember in Chapter 2 we discussed that your credit rating can be reviewed by many different entities such as landlords, utility companies, banks, insurance companies, professional licensing organizations, credit companies, and sometimes employers. Don't let poor credit tarnish your relationship or business transactions with any of these entities.

How to reduce your credit card debt.

Return what you can.

What did you buy with your credit cards that can still be returned? The obvious stuff would be something still in the box or packaging and within return deadlines published by the retailer you purchased from. What is hanging in your closet with the tags still on? If you haven't used a purchase yet, there is a good chance you didn't need it to begin with.

Renegotiate terms.

An excellent way to reduce your interest rate or monthly payment is to pick up the phone and call the credit card issuer. You will find that they are generally very open to working with you once you have explained your situation. The credit card company doesn't want you to default on your payment obligation. No one wins if that happens. Don't be afraid to be direct and specific in your requests. Ask for better terms, lower payments, a deferment, or whatever makes good financial sense for your personal situation.

Transfer your balances.

Can you transfer your balances to a lower interest card? If you
don't have a lower interest card or a credit card company wants
to charge you a fee for transferring talk to your banker. Tell her
what you are trying to accomplish and ask for solutions she may
have that can help you.

Groceries

In November 2010 I wrote about the dramatic price increases
being seen in raw goods, which included both manufacturing
materials, such as cotton, and food goods, such as corn and
wheat. In February 2011 the media began reporting sharp
increases in prices of manufactured goods, clothing, and food.
The raw materials price increases noticed 4 months earlier where
translating into more expensive finished goods.

Grocery prices will rise, but that should not affect how you eat.
Low income and more costly food prices meant switching to a diet
of ramen noodles years ago. Today, however, you don't have to
sacrifice a healthy and plentiful diet when your income is reduced.

Stephanie Nelson's story

There are plenty of ways to save on groceries, but you may want
to learn more about the Coupon Mom's three step approach to
cutting grocery costs. Extreme couponer, Stephanie Nelson, also
known as "The Coupon Mom" says 1) know how your grocery
store's savings program works, 2) know where to find the best
coupons, and 3) know when to use your coupons. The
CouponMom.com website is a wealth of information about saving
money on groceries. She also has coupon databases and an

instruction guidebook for finding the best deals time after time in grocery and drug stores.

Phones

This one seems to be real hard for younger people. You don't need a phone with all kinds of bells, whistles, and ringtones. (Even if you weren't unemployed) you don't need to pay for texting, gaming, watching TV or videos, emailing, or surfing the web. Of course, there will be those that that want to tell you their phone is a work tool that makes them ultra-efficient, allowing them to find jobs and deals. Bologna.

You need a phone for work, not fun. You are not going to text a job interviewer. You don't have time to game. You should be actively calling for work instead of watching YouTube on your phone. Cancel any extra service you are paying for, other than making a phone call, as soon as you can. If you have access to an internet connection you can get all those for free.

Clothing

Clothing is an expense that is harder to eliminate, simply because kids get bigger and everyone's clothes and shoes eventually wear out. Clothing costs can be affected by raw material costs to manufacturers, new styles, and the seasons, for example.

Timing your purchases makes the biggest difference if you are shopping for new clothes and shoes. Generally, there are huge clothing discounts on Black Friday and at the very end of each season. For instance, you will find much lower prices on summer clothing at the very end of summer!

Many people find high quality bargains at thrift stores such as those operated by Goodwill Industries. Another option for those in need of new clothes for work are charities such as Dress For Success in Pittsburgh, Pennsylvania.

Utilities

Here is a quick way to reduce your energy use: follow Jimmy Carter's example and not the one set by Barack Obama! On his first full day in office Barack Obama was photographed without a suit jacket on in the Oval Office. Why? President Obama hates the cold and had the temperature of the White House turned up!

Jimmy Carter's heating bill.

On the other hand, Jimmy Carter, who was often seen wearing a sweater in the White House, stated in 1977, "….and the last thing I'm doing is to ask everyone to cut down very strictly on the temperatures within homes. The whole White House is maintained at a temperature of 65 degrees. When you get a couple hundred people in a small room like this, the temperature goes up. But every thermostat in the White House, every thermostat in all Government buildings in this country are now set at 65 degrees, which is about 10 degrees lower. And if everybody will do that in private homes as well, and even cut back a little more at night, then that will make up half the shortage of natural gas--just that one thing."

A problem you run into while unemployed and wanting to reduce your utility bills by making your home more energy efficient, is that there is a cost to updating energy efficiency. The cost of new energy efficient windows, doors, and appliances can be out of reach for the unemployed.

One fairly inexpensive way to lower your electricity bill is to replace your incandescent light bulbs with compact fluorescent light bulbs. Many utility companies offer great financial incentives to offset the cost of replacing all the bulbs in your home.

Rather than focusing on the bigger items conduct a home energy audit or ask your utility companies to do it for you. Make a note of all the items that are using energy even though you are not using the item. You may find many "phantom energy users" throughout your home, such as, computer equipment left on, appliances plugged in, and adapters that come with rechargeable battery-powered cordless phones, cell phones, digital cameras and music players, power tools, and other electronic devices.

Another reason to get out of the house.

One suggestion I have for keeping your utility costs low is to get out of the house during the day, just like you would if you were going to work. Once you've been away from work for an entire month you will notice that your utility bills went up. Now that you are in the house longer the lights, heat, air, water, computer, etc., have all been used more.

At the very least, why not go spend the majority of your day working at the library? Take your laptop and set up your own "office" at one of the tables. Take a look at the proposed schedule in Chapter 4. Nearly all of that can happen at the library and on the road. Save money by shutting things off at home, and let the library heat and cool you while you work.

Transportation

Most people will go right to the gas prices when they think about cutting transportation costs, but guess what, even with all the right maintenance there is little you can do, except stop driving, to dramatically cut your fuel costs. Rather than focus on the fuel, think about the wear and tear on your car.

Not only is there the cost of replacement parts, but the labor costs can be as high as $90.00 per hour for someone to work on your car! Rodney was in hurry to get his 6 year old daughter to dance class. He took a shortcut, even though he knew about the extreme potholes on this particular route. The car bounced up and down, much to his daughter's delight, as Rodney raced to get to the class on time! One pothole was filled with water and gave a misleading indication of its true depth. Rodney hit it and immediately broke a tie rod end. He didn't make it to the class on time, had to have his vehicle towed, and pay a large repair bill.

Of course you should combine trips, car pool, and drive under 55, but also treat your car carefully. Premature or unnecessary breakdowns will cost you.

Taxes

Cosmo Kramer: It's a write-off for them.
Jerry Seinfeld: How is it a write-off?
Kramer: They just write it off.
Jerry: You don't even know what a write-off is.
Kramer: Do you?
Jerry: No, I don't.
Kramer: But they do, and they're the ones writing it off.

There are plenty of resources available to you to talk about tax deductions. Having a professional tax preparer listen to your particular situation and review your records and earnings will often pay for itself many times over by eliminating errors and finding additional deductions you may not have been aware of.

For the average person who is unemployed or an employee of someone else, there are far fewer deductions available than for business owners. Self-employment may be an option for some people for a variety of reasons, including using the tax advantages business owners enjoy. In the next chapter we will explore many of the reasons to start a part time business as well as the easiest ways to get your ideas off the ground. We will also discuss the SEA program and when it is ok to collect unemployment payments and be self-employed at the same time.

Key Takeaway: There are many ways to save money and get a better value for your money. Assess each area of your budget and seek out new ways to do better.

Insurance Secrets and Savings

During a time when money is tight it can be tempting to start cutting out expenses that on the surface don't seem to be adding much value to your day to day existence. Insurance is often such a target. You may have been paying your premiums for years, but have never had to use the insurance benefit. Now you are wondering if it is worth it to keep paying the premiums.

The fire at June Johns' home.

If you are tempted to reduce your costs by eliminating insurance consider this story. On Monday, January 31, 2011 June Johns and her family made it out of their burning home in Madison Heights, Virginia, just as the roof caved in. They had been trying to save money on heating oil by burning wood inside their home, which caused the house fire. The family did not have home insurance. They only possessions they had left were the contents of their garage and the clothes they were wearing at the time of the fire.

One of the larger expenses people have are the various insurances they purchases. Some of the basics you may have are renter/home, car, life, and disability. Within those general insurance areas are a variety of options that let you customize coverage to your particular needs. During a time when your household income is reduced it could be tempting to start trimming insurance coverage. There are several reasons why this is not a good idea.

There may not be any scientific proof that backs up Murphy's Law, but now is a bad time to put yourself at even more financial risk by reducing or eliminating insurance. Your intent of saving money is admirable, but bad things sometimes happen to good people. Generally speaking, the financial security the right insurance gives you is well worth the cost.

That doesn't mean you couldn't be doing better. Searching online will allow you to find many ways to arrange your lifestyle so that you can reduce your insurance premiums. However, two of the least talked about, but very important factors that determine your premiums are your credit rating and your loss history. In the following discussion, car insurance will be used as an example. However, the tips for reducing that insurance cost can be applied in other areas as well.

Insurance has always been a tool for managing risk and right now you are more at risk of catastrophic loss than ever before. Because your income has been dramatically reduced you are not going to be in a financially strong position from which to respond to events of loss. Losses from your home, transportation, and health are typically very expensive. Wind damaged rooftops, auto body repair, and emergency room visits cost much more than routine expenses you face.

Your life insurance policy is another policy you should reconsider canceling. Whether you have term or whole life insurance, you most likely have a guaranteed, locked in premium rate. Canceling your coverage and coming back later almost guarantees you will be quoted a higher premium.

If you are unemployed, you are already walking a tightrope balancing normal every day costs and your reduced income. The cost of one accident, without appropriate insurance protection, could be enough to push you down hard enough that you are unable to recover financially. That will have a negative impact on your quality of life for years to come.

Keeping appropriate amounts of home, auto, health, and life insurance should be a priority. If you are still concerned about the cost of maintaining insurance make an appointment with your insurance agent, explain your situation and your concerns, and ask for their professional advice and ideas for making the most out of your financial resources.

Health insurance.

If you had health insurance at the job you are laid off from the Consolidated Omnibus Reconciliation Act (COBRA) gives you the option to continue the policy you had at work, but at your own expense. If you are in a position to pay the full premiums that you will now be responsible for, you should keep the medical insurance. Without insurance coverage you are at a great risk for assuming extreme, life-changing debt because of an accident or serious illness.

For many people the amount you have to pay through COBRA is unmanageable. Perhaps, while working full-time, your employer was paying 60% of your $300.00 per month premium. Now, your income has been reduced 40%, for example, and you are responsible for 100% of the insurance premium, now $500.00. If you simply can't afford it, and don't qualify for other forms of free insurance through the state, you need to invest in preventative healthcare.

Knowing that one visit or stay at a hospital can wipe your savings out you should invest in maintaining your physical health. Exercise, eat right, stop smoking, don't work on the roof, wear a seat belt, don't dive in the shallow end of the pool, etc. Be careful and vigilant. Don't wait for a problem or accident to find you, look for them and take preventative/precautionary measures to avoid them.

Insurance Secret Number One.

All of us don't pay the same rate. "What? That's the secret? Tell me something I didn't know. Of course my rate is better than my 16 year old son who is driving a red sports car, and I am sure it is better than my neighbor who has been arrested twice for drunk driving. Hello!"

Well, that isn't quite it. Rates are typically determined by a number of factors. Insurance companies have proprietary formulas that are based on actuarial science that allows them to evaluate the risk you represent. That amount of risk will determine the rate you are quoted. So the real secret is the number of factors in the formula. You want to be sure you are "ranking" favorably for each factor. Yes, your age, number and type of tickets you've received, and type of vehicle you drive are items in the formula. However, even if you are doing all the usual things we are told to do, like wearing a seatbelt, you may still be paying more than your neighbor who is also doing those same things. Here is why.

Insurance Secret Number Two: getting a better rate also depends on your loss history and credit rating.

Just listen to the commercials. Safe drivers are actively sought after and wooed with better deals. Remember Allstate advertising a "Safe Driver Bonus Check"? Don't have an accident and they would send YOU a check. Everyone knows that safe drivers cost less, but how does an insurance company know that you are going to be a safe driver in the future? How will they forecast what you as an individual will typically cost them and thus determine how much to charge you? They discovered that two reports, which are part of their risk assessment formula, will help them predict your future behavior.

Loss history reports.

Also known as a loss history exchange report, it lists the number of insurance claims you have had and their details, such as the cost of the claim. This information becomes part of the equation that determines the rate you will be charged by a particular insurance company.

There are two loss history exchanges you should be aware of. These exchanges are the Automated Property Loss Underwriting Service (A-Plus) and the Comprehensive Loss Underwriting Exchange (CLUE). These exchanges collect information about your insurance claim history and make that information available to insurance companies who are considering what rates to quote you. Obviously, you want the information to be accurate, as incorrect information could make you appear to be a higher risk. Along with other factors, such as your credit report, these reports will be part of the formula that determines 1) if you can be insured and 2) what your rate will be.

Where does the data come from for the loss history exchange reports?

These companies get their information from insurance companies that supply them with your insurance and claim history data. Nearly all insurance companies report this data. These exchanges also provide a service to insurance companies by "providing information on current and previous coverages and other policy-level data".

The Comprehensive Loss Underwriting Exchange provides information such as your personal property damage claims, auto loss and claims history. Have you ever called your insurance agent, told them about a loss, and then decided not to submit a claim? Perhaps, you decided not to submit the claim because of the amount you would pay for a deductible. That inquiry can be reported to the Comprehensive Loss Underwriting Exchange, and may become part of your record. The fact that you are asking about a particular coverage could then be construed as you believing you have a possible upcoming claim – an insurance red flag.

Like credit reports you are entitled to a free report from each of these exchanges every 12 months. If you find errors on your insurance exchange report be sure to take the same steps you would when correcting errors on your credit report. Notify the exchange in writing and provide documentation backing up your claim.

How do I get a copy of my own loss history exchange report?

You can reach Automated Property Loss Underwriting Service at the A-PLUS Consumer Inquiry Center's 1-800-709-8842 phone number, option 2. You can reach Comprehensive Loss Underwriting Exchange at 1-866-312-8076.

Insurance & your credit history.

Insurance isn't much different from the credit card or car loan offers you will receive, in that your credit history is a determining factor in the rates you receive. One reason given by insurance representatives, when asked why credit history is used in the risk assessment, sounds much like that given by employers who check credit. A documented history of making on time payments and avoiding debt represents a pattern of responsible behavior. That pattern of responsible behavior could indicate responsible behavior in other areas, such as safe driving for example.

Insurance companies have no real need to look at your credit again after you have become their customer. However, if you add someone on to your policy, (perhaps you got married), they may want to check the credit history of that person.

If you haven't shopped around for better insurance rates in the last couple of years, (and after looking at your credit report, you've verified that your credit rating has improved) then shop around. Even ask your current broker for a better rate. Explain that your credit record has improved and you would like to have your rate re-evaluated.

If you want better insurance prices. get copies of your loss history report and your credit report. Be sure all of the information you find on these reports is accurate, otherwise take steps to make the appropriate corrections. When you have cleaned up the factors that affect your rates, go ahead and shop around for better insurance deals. However, remember that sometimes the best deals are close to home. Talk to your current insurance agent and tell her what your new situation is and what your goals are. Get insight on discounts you qualify for or steps you can take to improve the rate you get.

How To Pay Less Than The Other Guy

Chapter 1 mentioned you shouldn't be afraid to tell people you lost your job. This is a good lead in to reducing your bills. For example, ask your landlord if you can deduct $50.00 a month from your rent if you cut the grass or sweep the hallways each day. Ask the manager at your gym if you can come in early and help clean up in trade for a reduction in your monthly dues.

Think of all the people you pay each month and what you could offer in trade for a reduction in the amount you owe. Anyone can figure out that if you have lost your job you will have a lot less money to work with and that means they could possibly lose your business altogether. Create a win-win situation for both parties through negotiation where they give you a temporary discount and you give something up as well.

How Sandy Brady gets a discount.

Ever hear "It doesn't hurt to ask"? Sandy Brady sure had, and with one question she saved some money. Sandy was ready to purchase new windows for her home. She had several estimates done, and on the final one she got a price she liked. However, when she was sitting at her kitchen table with the salesman reviewing the estimate, she asked him a question she always asked salespeople, "Your estimate is close to the number I had in mind. How can I get a discount?" Sandy stated, "I used to be embarrassed to ask for money off of a purchase. I just accepted the price that was on a sticker or tag. However, when I saw a friend of mine routinely getting price reductions, just by asking for them, I decided I had nothing to lose."

Sandy is not alone. According to an article on the WTAE website, Duquesne University marketing professor Audrey Guskey says there is a great chance you can do the same. Guskey said consumer surveys back up her haggling success and that she encourages more shoppers to do so. "Only one in eight people haggle, so it's a very low number, but about 50 percent of those haggling actually get what they're asking for. They get a much better deal," said Guskey.

Can you guess what some of the secrets to successful haggling are? For starters, doing your homework by comparing prices puts you in a better position to negotiate, because you know what a retailer's competitor is charging. Also the article states that persistence, politeness, and being prepared with information pays off.

In Sandy's case, after asking for a discount, the salesman called his manager and then responded that he was authorized to give her an additional 15% off if she was ready to sign the contract and pay that day. That was a discount the salesman had not mentioned earlier. In Sandy's case that meant an additional $450.00 off the sale price the window company was already offering. "Why would I hesitate to ask for a discount? The window company wants the business and I need windows. Giving me that discount meant getting my business. We both win in the end.", said Sandy.

Key Takeaway: Only 1 in 8 people will ask for a discount, but the one person who does has a 50% chance of getting exactly what they ask for!

Are you paying fractional premiums?

Fractional premiums are additional amounts of money you are paying because you are making payments versus paying for an item all at once. When was the last time you asked a salesman for a discount when paying up front for something? Perhaps the seller would be willing to give you a discount for paying cash rather than paying a fee to a lender or waiting months for the full payment.

You may not always get additional money off, but you may be in a position to get a better deal, such as additional product for the same amount of money. Avoid fractional premiums and use your ability to negotiate and pay up front to your advantage by leveraging that into an additional discount.

Key Takeaway: Pay up front and save big.

The Cost Of Your Health

A story, aired on "The Wall Street Journal This Morning" radio program on December 28, 2010, quoted economists who used a government survey called the Behavioral Risk Factor Surveillance System. The economists in the story concluded that for every percent of increase in any state's unemployment rate "the people who are most prone to be unemployed eat 2-4% less fruits and vegetables and 8% less salad." While the economists conducting the study couldn't produce a conclusive answer as to why that was true the fact remains that those people were eating less fruits, vegetables, and salad.

Eating fruit, vegetables, and salads is not the only factor in maintaining your health, but the overall point brought to light by this study is important. Whether you are employed or not, your health will play a major role in your finances and quality of life. Poor health comes with varying degrees of tangible and intangible costs. From a financial aspect there is medicine, office visits, specialists, and tests, for example. Other costs to you can include lower energy, depression, and your time as you deal with the illness. Poor health is just another drag on your ability to work through an already harder time. Taking measures to prevent sickness, such as eating a healthy diet, is very important right now.

How you improve or maintain your health is up to you and your doctor, but of course there are basics that all of us should be aware of such as eating right, exercising, and eliminating unsafe habits. Not that having health insurance should have been a reason to allow your health slide in the first place, but you may or may not have the insurance at this point. Whether you do or don't, there are additional costs to you any time you need medical attention. There has never been a better time to eliminate and avoid those costs.

One other note on the study mentioned above. They also reported that people who were working tended to smoke more than those that were not working. Again, no explanation was given telling us why. However, smoking is a great example of a habit that has tangible and intangible costs.

According to the website TobaccoFreeKids.org the 2010 national average cost of a pack of cigarettes is $5.51, but that price can vary widely by state, due to their particular tobacco tax rate. If you are a smoker or live with a smoker, have you ever played the trade game? If you didn't smoke, what could you buy instead? If you smoke just one pack per day that is about $165.00 per month. It is difficult to put an exact price tag on the unseen health consequences of smoking, but we do know how much it will cost to buy the cigarettes. Would $165.00 come in handy right now? What are your other habits costing you?

Take a look at your eating and exercising habits. Both are crucial to the energy you need for finding new work, as well as, minimizing health care costs during a time of reduced income.

There are plenty of resources online and at the library, for instance, that can provide you will tips and information on how to stay healthy and out of the doctor's office. However, one comment I would like to make is that momentum can carry you forward or backward. If you sit still in front of a screen all day you are creating backward momentum for your health. You will begin to feel lethargic and that spills over into other areas of your life. Get up, move around, and don't be afraid to break a sweat!

Key Takeaway: Poor health is a financial disaster waiting to happen when you are unemployed. Take action to regain or maintain your good health!

Health fairs and wellness screenings.

At any given time during the year there are many free health fairs you can attend and receive preventative health care completely free. No insurance or money on your part is needed to benefit from the various services that community health practitioners provide at these forums. This gives you a fantastic opportunity to keep up with basic medical care and monitoring just like you would have when your income was higher.

Duquesne University in Pittsburgh is an example of one of many colleges that provide free wellness screenings to the community. Sponsored by the university's Center For Pharmacy Care and funded by charitable donations, Duquesne's program provides many medical services whose cost would normally be out of reach for those looking for work. Simply by calling and making an appointment you can request any of these services, for example:

-Cholesterol screening

-Diabetes and serum glucose screening

-Facial skin analysis

-Bone density testing

-Anemia screening

-Body composition analysis

-and many other free services.

Heath fairs bring multiple health professionals together in one location all at once. Many are free and simply provided to the community as a public service. Take advantage of these opportunities!

At many health fairs you'll find medical staff who are performing more specialized (and costly) screenings for free. For example, you can free screenings for free screening for HIV, prostate cancer, hypertension, Hepatitis C, MRSA, and diabetes. Dental exams are sometimes provided at health fairs. Testing can include mammograms, blood lipids, body composition, and EKGs. At some health fairs you may get a spinal adjustment by a chiropractor, a short massage, acupuncture treatment, or even a free healthy meal.

Christmas & Birthday Giving

Christmas time can be a stressful time even if you are working. It is often written about in *The Quarter Roll* because year after year it is like we see two Christmases. There is the Christmas portrayed in It's A Wonderful Life, in the Coca-Cola commercials, and in the pictures on Christmas cards. Then there is the number of people who associate Christmas with financial hardship.

One of my "favorite" stories of Christmas is the year a friend and I had just finished decorating our apartment. We sat down to relax for a bit. The apartment looked great, and with all the decorations, lights, and tree the entire atmosphere of the apartment had changed. It had a festive, yet relaxed and homey look. It really was a great time of year. We all had a steady income, reliable transportation, good health, and no serious economic concerns. It looked like this would be a great Christmas.

So why was my friend sitting there crying? I asked her what could possibly be wrong; I thought everything was great. She told me that now she thinking about shopping for Christmas gifts. I discovered that she had been worried about gift money for months, and now that Christmas was weeks away she was feeling overwhelmed and depressed. She felt that she was $400.00 short of what she needed in order to get everyone great gifts! For her, Christmas time was a financial nightmare.

That moment has always stuck with me, and I think about it often during the holidays. She wasn't the first, or even last person, I've seen stress over Christmas gift money. In fact it's almost a given that somebody you know will be stressed over money during the holidays, and honestly, I have seen the same thing happen with birthdays. Is that really what the holidays and birthdays are supposed to be about?

You simply can not fall into this thought pattern. There are plenty of ways to celebrate Christmas without spending money. If the calendar said August 12 instead of December 25, would you need money in order to show someone you appreciate and love them? Make a commitment that you will invest time, instead of money, to create no cost or low cost ways to celebrate the holidays.

In *The Quarter Roll* article "12 Better Days of Christmas" there were many suggestions on how to celebrate a frugal and fun Christmas. Some suggestions were giving your time instead of money, using pictures to create unforgettable holiday memories and gifts, and writing a letter instead of giving a store bought card. One of the best stories was this one.

White elephant gift giving – one man's old boots is boy's dream come true.

The best gifts are not always new, but may come with lots of mileage and loaded with character. Everyone's sense of value is different. That gift you find may be old, but perhaps it is perfect for the person you want to give it to because this gift packs lots of nostalgia, completes a collector's masterpiece, or even replaces a long lost memory.

After 7 year old Mike's first school field trip to the fire station, he desperately wanted to be a fireman! During the trip he got to sit in the fire trucks, use the sirens and lights, and even turn on the alarm at the station. He was very excited about pretending to be a fireman for the day.

At Christmas his parents gave him a fireman's gently used boots and coat along with a toy fireman helmet. Mike thought he had died and gone to heaven, and reacted accordingly. Of course, the boots and coat did not fit, and Mike's parents had bought what was basically garbage to the firefighters for a tiny donation to the volunteer fire department, but that didn't matter to Mike. He had real fireman equipment and you couldn't have bought him a better gift.

The National Holiday For The Unemployed

Exodus 10:15 "For they covered the face of the whole earth, so that the land was darkened; and they did eat every herb of the land, and all the fruit of the trees which the hail had left: and there remained not any green thing in the trees, or in the herbs of the field.........."

What is the first thing you think of when you picture Black Friday in your mind? You might picture the same images the news media waits all night long to capture and then play repeatedly on the evening news. Swarms of pushy shoppers shoving their way past the store employees at the front door and descending on merchandise like hungry locust on a cornfield, mercilessly consuming everything in sight.

If you are unemployed, I would like to suggest that you consider Black Friday a holiday, because the cost of so many things is dramatically reduced for a few hours on this day. What you couldn't afford to replace in your home before, now may be available at a far lower price.

Even though many people write off Black Friday as a day the "crazies" come out of the woodwork at 4 in the morning to buy a cheap video game, you will see why Black Friday offers a once a year chance to buy the things you need for your home, but now with a lot less money.

Black Friday crowds.

There can be a lot of excited energy in the crowd, and seasoned Black Friday shoppers can easily spot the rookies with their wide eyes and fidgety anticipation. If you have been through enough Black Fridays, you can identify three distinct groups of shoppers. One of these groups can show you how to save substantial amounts of money all year long, a valuable insight during times of reduced income. Let's take a look at how this one particular day, if used properly, will lower your overall budgetary needs all year long.

Poking around.

The excitement of Black Friday is what attracts the first group of people to the stores. They are there to people watch, poke around the store for nothing in particular, and perhaps go get some breakfast with a friend. They have no real agenda and will most likely be texting pictures and observations about the things they've seen.

Gift shopping.

The second group is here for gifts. Gifts for others and of course, a gift or two for themselves. According to the November 20, 2010 Suze Orman personal finance show, holiday shoppers would spend an average of $689.00 during the holiday season. They will also spend an additional $107.50 on themselves. This group is ready to buy clothes, toys, decorations, gadgets, and jewelry. They have a list of people they want to buy for and where the deals are.

The strategists.

The third group of people is here because they have been strategically planning needed purchases during the past year, and forecasting their household needs for the upcoming year as well. During the year you have been watching your household needs very closely.

You know that the kids will need new clothes and shoes, the microwave is not working anymore, and your vacuum has lost all its' cleaning ability. You may need to replace appliances, tools, bedding, automotive parts and tires, cookware, dishware, and clothing.

Black Friday is an excellent time to buy the things you typically need throughout the year, but at substantially lower costs. Putting off purchases of these things, or buying them now knowing they are going to need replaced in the next several months, will give you additional purchasing firepower you certainly wouldn't have had at regular or normal sale prices.

Maximizing the value of this day depends on how well you have planned and budgeted ahead of time. Keep track of your household needs throughout the year. If something can be repaired versus replaced assess the value of each option. If you know you will be in a position where you need to buy necessities, budget some money for Black Friday.

Strategy: Be sure to look for combinations of deals. For example, Pittsburgh grocer Giant Eagle, sold gift cards from 100s of retailers at face value, but gave customers an incentive of gasoline discounts based on dollar amount of the gifts cards they purchased. If your kids need new winter coats, and the $50.00 coats were on sale for $20.00 each at JCPenny, you could buy JCPenny gift cards at Giant Eagle, get the associated gasoline discount, and buy the dramatically reduced winter coats with the gift cards.

Would you rather shop online than at the store? Millions of people do, but note that the online assortment of deals has traditionally not been as complete as those found at the brick and mortar stores. That doesn't mean you can't find good options on the web. If you do shop online be sure to search for discount codes and coupons prior to completing your purchase.

Key Takeaway: Black Friday is another option for finding dramatic savings on necessities for your home and family, but do your homework and plan ahead in order to maximize your time and money.

Chapter 4

Investing in you and your things

Chapter Overview

In this chapter we will discuss many ways to invest in yourself that will allow you to enjoy more personal fulfillment and make yourself more valuable in the marketplace. Your time on unemployment is an opportunity to invest in yourself and lead a more fulfilling lifestyle, further your education, regain your physical or emotional health, and obtain new marketable skills that lead to higher paying jobs.

Your New Daily Schedule

"I think the harder you work, the more luck you have."
-R. David Thomas

Most likely your workplace had set a schedule for you and you were managing the scraps of time that were left over. Now, it is up to you to effectively manage your time. Your first thought might be that you will have plenty of time to both search for a job and catch up on many of the personal distractions you have been missing out on, such as growing your Farmville crops or completing your World of Warcraft quest.

Actually, your new daily schedule will be more intense than the schedule at your previous job. As mentioned before, you don't have a day to spare in the race to preserve the lifestyle unemployment wants to rip from you.

The following list only includes basics that should be included in the structure of your day. It is based on a 16 hour day (you get 8 hours for sleeping and the weekends are yours to do as you please – see the section on travel later on in this chapter). Although not all of the 16 hours look like they are directly job search related, they do support your efforts in some way. For example, exercising and eating right may not directly get you a new job, but being healthy will minimize your risk of health related costs and keep your energy and focus high while you actively pursue new work. If you identify other activities that will directly influence your success in finding a job you should work those into your new schedule as well.

1. Looking for work (6 hours per day).

"Battles are won before they are fought." Sun Tzu

Obviously, replacing your income is your new job and your number one priority. The biggest mistake you can make is to believe that you can mail, or email, 20 resumes out first thing in the morning and then be done for the rest of the day. The only thing that will come of that is 20 employers' garbage cans will be a little fuller.

During this portion of your day you want to strategize. Job hunting is much more than blindly sending 100 resumes out each week. You want to create a structured plan that supports your goal of finding new work.

Dan Miller, from 48days.com, suggests that you first create a list of 40-50 companies that you would like to work for. Once you have created that list learn as much as you can about each company. Who are the decision makers? Who do you know who works there or knows someone who works there? Have your toured their facility? Do you know what their current needs are? What do you know about the industry in which they do business? That research will be part of the 7 hours you spend each day looking for work.

Having a thorough understanding of your target companies will put you in a much stronger position for determining the best way to get their attention. When you do get their attention you will be just as versed on the company as someone who has already been working there. That will give you favorable hiring preference over someone who knows little about the company.

"Even if you've had your resume professionally written, one size does not fit all in this extremely competitive job search market." HarveyCareers.com

Part of your day should be writing appropriate resumes. One general resume will not be sufficient when applying to a variety of employers. Even if you are applying to two companies from the same industry you may need to customize your resume.

Matt Damon's story.

Remember, customization is not deception. Lying will work against you as demonstrated in this story about actor Matt Damon. In a June 2011 Boston Herald article Damon admitted he had lied at a job interview when trying to get into the entertainment business.

A TV producer needed someone who could ice skate and Damon, who could not skate, told the hiring manager he could do it. Damon, who ruined the show and injured himself in the process stated, "My first professional acting job was for WCVB-TV. Dick Albert had a show called, 'Use Your Smarts', and I did a vignette where I played a young Michael J. Fox – and I had to ice skate. I fell and knocked myself out. So my first job ever I actually cost the production money because I lied in my audition and couldn't skate."

You aren't going to put things on your resume that are not true. Customization is simply creating a unique presentation of your work history that makes more sense to the particular company you are applying to.

A customer service supervisor does a lot of things including answering phones. New Company A wants someone to answer phones and talk to customers, not necessarily supervise others. The unemployed customer service supervisor should primarily highlight her experience answering phones, more than the fact that she was a supervisor with other duties.

How do you know what to put on your customized resume? The easiest thing to do is research the company you are applying to. What words / industry jargon do they use? What skills and experience did they specifically ask for in the job posting?

Highlight areas of your experience they would be most interested in, not necessarily the stuff you are most proud of. Match the content of your resume to the specifics that company is looking for. Talk in their language.

Save all of your customized resumes into a portfolio of resumes. This will make creating new resumes easier as you can take pieces of various resumes to create a new one. Also, it will allow you to retrieve the resume you sent to an employer and walk the hiring manager through it when you both meet.

Still not sure how to write resumes? Attend a resume writing class. Most community colleges offer resume writing classes at a low cost. It is a good investment. Hiring managers that see poorly written resumes will just throw them out. Your resume is a reflection of you and you want it to look good. Would you stand at an employer's door with your shirt tails hanging out, messy hair, and stains on your pants? Don't let your resume look like that either!

Make personal visits.

"You can't just sit behind a desk all the time and think you know what is going on in the world. You have to go out and see it for yourself. You got to smell it. You got to taste it. You got to see it."
– Anderson Cooper

No matter how perfect your resume looks it will never look better than you. Resumes don't have personality. You do. Resumes can't personally interact with the particular characteristics of a hiring manager. You can. Like the quote above suggests, recruiters need to *see* you. Your online profile or resume may be just slightly different than what the hiring manager is looking for, but meeting you in person could help her see the real value you bring.

That is why another part of your day should include leaving the house and looking for work in person. Personally drop off resumes after you have done your homework on the company. This will show initiative. Additionally, since you are already in the building there is a good chance someone will take a few minutes to talk to you. What a great opportunity to get some face time other candidates will not get.

2. Networking (2 hours per day).

Leaning on your professional network is one of the best ways to find a new job. Rather than depending only on your own efforts to find a job, enlist the help of all the people you know. Wouldn't it be better to have 50 people looking for a job for you versus one? There are many ways you can reach out to others and expand your professional network. Spend this portion of the day staying in touch with other professionals and building a rapport with others in the industry you wish to work in.

Dolly Madison's networking tip.

This former first lady may have been best known for making sure the portrait of George Washington was saved on August 24, 1814, minutes before the British army arrived at the White House steps intent on destroying the first family's home with fire. However, Dolly Madison was a master networker and had one particularly unique networking strategy.

Mrs. Madison would regularly write letters to prominent women across the country and ask them for recipes she could use in the White House. Of course, these influential women were flattered that they were asked for their recipes, but it was Dolly who won friend after friend with her recipe networking! When it was time for her husband, James Madison, to campaign for a second term, Dolly was sure to ask her new recipe sharing friends for their support in reelecting her husband.

Networking isn't just sending an email to everyone you know and asking them to let you know of any jobs they hear about. And it certainly isn't about updating your Facebook page with your weekend activities.

Some ways to grow your network are attending a free business seminar each week or checking your local paper, chamber of commerce, library, or community college websites for listings of such events. Send an email of congratulations to someone who was promoted in your industry. You can find those people in the business listings in the newspaper. Reach out to people you used to work with but have lost contact. LinkedIn is a great forum for that.

The local unemployment office is another great place to network. Employers are often invited throughout the month to set up recruiting days at the unemployment office. The unemployment office will also hold training classes on a variety of topics. Any event the unemployment office holds gives you is an opportunity to meet new people and improve your work skills at the same time.

3. Your Health (2 hours).

Tired of being constantly tired and unmotivated, Kelly Osbourne, daughter of Ozzy Osbourne, started exercising and eating better early in 2010. During the next 12 months she lost over 50 pounds. Not only did she look better and have more energy, but Osbourne also noted that she felt more confident and was in a much better mood. She noted, "….exercising gets my endorphins going and really lifts my mood."

Your physical and psychological health is the engine behind your job search. Like Kelly Osbourne noted before her physical transformation, if you are always tired and unmotivated you just won't want to get up and make good things happen for yourself. Your health is directly linked to the amount of energy, focus, and stamina you will need for the work ahead. Poor health is a burden that will just weigh you down.

Of course, there may be an ailment, such as diabetes, that is out of your control and will require regular maintenance and your attention, regardless of how hard you work at maintaining your health. However, these 2 hours of your day should be devoted to improving your overall health.

Health isn't just about feeling and looking good. Your good health is also a cost control mechanism. Poor health has a financial cost and a productivity cost. Right now is not a good time to be faced with medical bills. Additionally, the stress brought on by poor health will only slow down your job hunting efforts.

4. Learn something new (2 hours per day).

"I don't think much of a man who is not wiser today than he was yesterday." Abraham Lincoln

Spending 1 hour per day learning something new will give you more to talk about to different employers. Learning something new will stimulate your creativity, give you new perspectives on solving problems, and increase your resourcefulness.

Where do you go to learn something new? Go help a friend fix something, go to the library, take a class at the community college, attend a public hearing in your municipality, or subscribe to a new informational podcast.

5. Your money (1 hour per day).

Money must have a slippery texture or great magician skills. It can easily slip right out of your hands and just vanish! That is why you need to be extra vigilant about where your money is going when you are unemployed. If you are not strategic about managing your expenses, and accounting for where each dollar goes, you can easily get into financial trouble.

Spend some time each day managing your money. That will include searching for bargains and better deals. You can do that by finding ways to get two meals out of ingredients rather than one meal.

5 year old Brooke's tenacity.

Brooke was a five year old who loved chocolate, but not ice cream. With the same attention to detail a crime scene investigator possesses, Brooke would meticulously comb through a bowl of ice cream just to find the last chocolate chip.

When she was done you could be assured that the bowl, still filled with ice cream, was free of any remnant of chocolate. This is the type of gusto with which you should sift through your day's/week's/month's expenses. That is how you should be micromanaging your expenses right now.

6. Your home (3 hours per day).

"I'm an organization freak. Cleaning out a drawer...makes me feel calm and sorted." - Actress Reese Witherspoon

Managing this portion of your day includes interacting with your family and friends in addition to creating a home environment that is conducive to supporting your job hunting focus.

Remember that you want each part of your life to support your goal of finding work. Like the Reese Witherspoon quote above implies, a neat, clean, and organized home can help give you a calm and serene feeling that will allow you to focus more strongly on job hunting.

Albert Einstein once described the three rules of work he followed:

1. Out of clutter find simplicity

2. From discord find harmony

3. In the middle of difficulty lies opportunity.

A messy room creates silent chaos. What happens when an alarm clock goes off? The abrupt loudness of an alarm clock does exactly what it is intended to do: create an attention grabbing distraction in the room so your focus on sleep is broken. A messy home won't be loud like an alarm clock, but the distractions it creates can be very similar.

Cleaning your home, even if you just reorganize furniture, can give you a refreshing feeling. That is a good mind set to be in when you go to work on your goals. Perhaps, just starting with organizing your home you will find simplicity, harmony, and opportunity!

Your family and friends.

Not everyone has supportive family members or loyal friends, even though these people would be invaluable to you for emotional support during a trying time, such as time spent in unemployment.

The best thing you can do is work on building a core group of people in your life that you know will be honest with you and with whom you can have meaningful and supportive interactions. Rather than concerning yourself if that person is a family member or lifelong friend, seek to build that relationship with anyone who fits the mold.

When you meet someone who you can relate to it doesn't matter if they are former co-workers, neighbors, fellow gym members, grandkids, or the cashier at the grocery store. Build that relationship.

Organizing your records.

We just talked about the virtue of keeping a neat and organized home. It eliminates clutter that seems to reach its invisible hands into your day and keep you distracted from your work. One particular area you should get organized is your financial records. This will allow you to create a more accurate budget, based on what you are actually spending, not just what you think you are spending. A good place to start is by saving and reviewing your receipts.

Do you save your receipts? Do you even ask for a receipt when purchasing something? The article "Price Protection Plans: Save Cash By Saving Receipts" on WPXI.com made a great point about retailers who will pay you the difference in price if a competitor advertises the item you bought for a lower amount.

Collecting a price match is one very good reason for saving your receipts. However, can you think of any others?

More reasons to save your receipts.

1. Warranties. When you file a claim for your product's warranty you will most likely be asked for a copy of the original receipt in order to receive service.

2. Recordkeeping. Having your receipts handy allows you to match up charges or debits from your checking account or credit cards.

3. Cash back. Many retailers will only issue store credit if you do not have the original receipt. If you want your money back you will need a receipt.

4. Proof of items purchased. If you receive a delivery that doesn't contain all the items you purchased your receipt will show what else you are entitled to.

5. Rebates. There are often rebates you qualify for, but retailers and manufacturers will want to see a copy of your receipt in order to complete the rebate.

6. Legal. If you are in the unfortunate position of having to prove your claims or rights about a product or service in court, a copy of your receipt could help make your case.

7. Taxes. When reviewing your organized receipts from the past year, you or your accountant may find additional expenses that can be deducted from your taxes.

Whether you keep all your receipts in separate folders, a safe, or an old shoebox, having those key records can save you many potential headaches and dollars.

Helping Your Things Age Gracefully

Regular maintenance of your assets is an excellent way to preserve your savings. By extending the useful life of the durable goods you own you free up money that would have normally been spent on replacements.

Refrigerators, jeans, shoes, cars, computers, phones, and the materials and fixtures that make up your home are examples of durable goods. Non-durable goods are food, medicine, gasoline, and electricity, for example. You can manage your use of non-durable goods, but they are gone forever as you consume them.

If you are unemployed it will hurt much more if you are hit with large replacement bills. Go around your home and make a list of the items that should receive regular maintenance. Remember that even small leaks around faucets, doors, and windows add up to wasted money.

Janice's expensive vacation.

Janice was an unemployed mail order goods supervisor. At home she noticed that the connecting tube from the wall to the toilet in her bathroom was leaking a little bit. She was trying to save money so opted not to immediately buy the $5.00 replacement connector. Instead, she put an old bowl under the drip and would empty it every couple of days.

Janice was leaving for several days to take care of her mother. She turned off the water to the connector, but left the bowl under it anyway. When Janice returned home 3 days later she saw a large wet spot on the garage ceiling.

She discovered that the valve in the wall that had been leaking was so old it was incapable of fully stopping the water from coming to the bathroom, even when turned off. The packing inside the valve had rotted away. The water that leaked out went through the bathroom floor and onto the garage ceiling below. While only a small drip, the water had enough time to cause $1,800.00 in damage.

The real value of home maintenance.

Extending the life of your home and the things in it makes sense, regardless of your employment situation. Basic repairs and maintenance will lower your yearly costs. If the typical life expectancy of your refrigerator is 14 years, but you get 20 years out of it you have saved money that can be used for something else.

Here are some examples of the typical life expectancies (in years) of items you will find around your home.

Microwaves	8 years
Ranges, electric	16
Ranges, gas	19
Ranges, hoods	14
Refrigerators, compact	8
Refrigerators, standard	14
Water heaters, electric	14

Water heaters, gas	9
Washers	12
Dryers, electric	14
Dryers, gas	13
Dishwashers	12
Food waste disposers	13
Freezers	16
Compactors	11

Source: MrAppliance.com

Aluminum siding	20-50
Carpeting	11
Exterior deck	15
Exterior paint	7-10
Garage door	20-50
Garage door opener	10
Veneer (brick, stone)	100+
Vinyl floor	20-30
Vinyl siding	50
Wood floor	100+
Wood siding	10-100

Source: ThisOldHouse.com

Don't think you have the right handyman skills to give your home regular maintenance? There are many resources available to help you.

1. The internet.

Websites such as Yahoo Answers, wikiHow, YouTube, and eHow are loaded with credible advice on repairing or performing routine maintenance on just about anything you can think of. You may have to sort through some of the amateur stuff, but there are lots of experts online who are willing to give you easy to understand, detailed instructions that will walk you through various home projects.

2. Building supply stores.

Home Depot and Lowes are just two building supply stores that offer regular training classes to the public for free. For example, The Home Depot Improver Club arranges training in their stores on skills such as deck staining, installing ceiling fans, home safety, painting, installing a sink, and even outdoor grilling.

3. Your community college.

Many community colleges offer non-credit classes for topics such as basic home repair, landscaping, and car repair. These classes may be up to several weeks long and can be much more in depth than the classes you find at home improvement stores.

Why You Should Travel, Go On Vacation & Get Out

A business reason to travel.

One of the very first lessons I learned when studying sales was taking a few quick seconds to scan someone's work area and look for something that you both had in common. It could be a kid's graduation picture, an autographed baseball, the name of a person / place / event, a diploma, or exotic plant. Whatever it was, even if your connection to it was minor, it could be used to build an instant bond with the other person. It is a lot easier to do this well if you are personally a well-rounded person.

Getting out and exploring the world is part of that process. Experiencing many new things gives you plenty of topics with which you can talk about with first-hand knowledge. Nothing builds rapport with a hiring manager faster than a personal anecdote about an interest of theirs.

A personal reason to travel.

If you are unemployed it doesn't mean you are not working. Creating income alternatives and increasing the value of your assets and yourself has become your full-time job. You will still be tired by the end of the week just like you used to be at your old job.

Getting away will allow you to recharge and come back to your work strong and focused. Having some time off from this new style of working will allow you to be more productive.

How to pay for travel when you are unemployed.

One of the most expensive expenditures many households wrestle with is their family vacation. There are many reasons why a family vacation is important. It is a time for the family to put aside all the typical daily distractions and spend time focusing on each other. It is a time to relax and get away from the grind of work. It can be a good time to recharge.

However, if you are unemployed, your traditional idea of a family vacation will need to change. As we will see, you can still take a vacation, several in fact. You can still gain many of the positive things from a vacation, but by reworking your ideas of how a vacation should look, you can get away for a fraction of what you used to pay.

Every year, millions of people travel to the usual vacation spots. Beaches, Washington, DC, and amusement parks are some examples of a typical get away. The problem is that there are lots of people and lots of expense. Some of the largest expenses come from simply getting there, lodging, and eating. Remember that the intent of the vacation is relaxation and recharging. Just like our discussion about Christmas time, when you have to spend a lot of money to do that, you are defeating the purpose.

VisitsByMaureen.com

The website VisitsByMaureen.com shows many examples of the various trips you can take that don't have many of the traditional costs associated with vacation trips. Maureen Smith, founder of the website, states that she is a person who likes to see and experience interesting places, but has little money to spend on travel costs.

Her goal is to find unique, out of the way spots that are within driving distance of her home and don't have the high costs associated with traditional fun spots like amusement parks, concerts, or theater productions.

Smith says, "What I discovered is that our country is loaded with hundreds of years of history that surrounds us and is available for us to enjoy. Not only that, but you will see that there are many free, yet interesting, places to visit." Smith used examples of free factory tours, niche museums, national parks close to home, and even Presidential museums as places that are inexpensive to visit, but loaded with things an entire family can enjoy.

Smith suggests combining discounts with these short, but action packed trips. "You will find that many of the out of the way spots are eager to attract more visitors to their site, and offer discounts and other ways to save. I often combine discounts and coupons with their low entry fees to get the absolute best deal." In some cases buying a membership to one museum will give you entry to many more museums for free. Smith also mentioned using an AAA discount and coupons found in the Entertainment Book.

How much does Smith pay for entrance to a baseball game? $6.00 at the Butler Blue Sox. For a day at the amusement park? $5.00 at Lakemont Park in Altoona. A visit to the historic Gallitzin Railroad Tunnels and Museum? $0.00!

Another advantage of a short trip away is you don't have that feeling of "needing a vacation after your vacation". Let's face it, sometimes getting away for 5-7 days is exhausting. The travel time, as well as the packing and unpacking, can just wear you out! Rather than taking one 6 day long vacation and traveling home tired, take 6 short one day trips and come home feeling refreshed.

Vacations will continue to be important to you and your family for a variety of reasons. How you create that vacation experience will need to change though. More frequent day trips will allow you to get away, spend time with your family, save the expense of traditional vacations, and experience new things you may not have even known were so close to home!

Key Takeaway: Short, inexpensive getaways are good for your state of mind. Find the deals, get refreshed, and come back ready to work even harder.

How To Make The Internet Sing Your Praises

"I really felt I had the ball. But it doesn't matter what I think."
– Troy Polamalu, Steelers cornerback

How do you learn about a new business you are considering spending money at? If you are like most people you use the web. You may search the company's website or other sites that discuss good, and even bad, experiences at the company in question. Just like we use the web to check out a business we may want to shop at, companies have discovered the web is an effective way to shop for employees as well.

It is no secret that many company recruiters checkout your online footprint as part of the interview process. It is not uncommon for them to look at your Facebook page, and other social sites, as well as simply doing a Google search on your name.

While you may think your online party pictures are cool, it really doesn't matter what you think. It is what the hiring managers think that counts. While many articles about this subject focus on cleaning up the skeletons in your virtual closet, why not use web technology to enhance your resume and sales pitch?

Ever sit in an interview and wish there was a way to demonstrate more of your work and accomplishments? A website allows you to design a presentation that showcases your achievements. It also can be fashioned to enhance your own personal brand. Even without a website there are plenty of web based sources that allow you to showcase your skills to the world.

Creating a professional website about yourself is extremely easy. There are many resources online that allow you to create your own webpage for free. Google owned Blogger is one such site. This site provides easy to follow, step by step instructions that allow you to create your own customized webpage and domain name. You can learn more about website resumes from John Williams' story in chapter 5.

Google yourself.

Speaking of Google, when was the last time you Googled yourself? You can bet a recruiter will. What do the top 10 results show? Put yourself in a hiring manager's shoes and ask "Are these results positive or negative?". What can you do to fill the top 10 search results with positive news and information about you? Find appropriate formats online that will allow you to put positive oriented news about yourself on the web. That is what you want Google to find and show to recruiters.

Key Takeaway: What can you find about yourself on the web? What will employers see? Craft your online reputation just like you would on your resume.

Why You Should Start A Business. Any Business.

There are many reasons to start your own part-time small business, especially if you are unemployed. Owning a small business doesn't take any formal training, and there is the potential to make extra money, meet new people, further develop your work skills, and decrease your tax liability.

Any extra income would certainly be helpful, if you are able to make a profit. "What? I may not make any money from my own small business?" That's right. Of course you will work hard at making money from your business, but don't plan on retiring with mounds of money any time soon. It is not uncommon for new business owners to need 2-3 years before making a profit. Even if you are initially unable to earn any money from your business there are still valid reasons to get started.

How you get business street smarts.

At a minimum, the mere act of going through the motions of a business start-up will allow you to gain new experience that makes you a more qualified job candidate. Managing the start-up phase of a new business is like earning an advanced degree in your profession. The experience you gain is highly marketable.

The start-up process for a new venture can be intense. Even if you are an expert in the field already, you're going to encounter many nuances in your industry you haven't worked through before.

For example, you may have been a facilities manager at a factory, but as a contractor your skills will be put to the test in a variety of new problems that need fixed. Now that you know how to work though those problems, you will be more valuable to an increasing number of employers.

You are still paying all those taxes?

Business owners have many more tax incentives available to them than other people. Just some of the many deductions available to small business owners are: repairs and maintenance, office equipment, licenses, office supplies, education, advertising, utilities, auto mileage, and a home office. Using a professional accountant ensures you are getting all the incentives you are entitled to.

You do need to make sure that your business isn't just a hobby. The IRS treats each differently. You can have a hobby where you try to make money, but the tax implications for deductions are much different than for full-time small businesses. One of the ways the IRS determines if you have a hobby versus a small business is to look for a profit from your business 3 out of the last 5 years.

Don't let this scare you off from starting your own "for profit" business. You just need to be able to demonstrate that you have been taken reasonable actions to generate profits. There is no penalty, from the IRS, for not making money, even if you haven't earned a profit 3 out of the last 5 years. If for some reason you are ever challenged by the IRS to explain why you are not generating a profit, just be ready to show the regular, meaningful actions you have taken to make money.

Spending $10,000.00 on crafting materials, and then visiting a flea market once a month, where you sell $20.00 worth of crafts is not a reasonable amount of effort.

Networking opportunities.

Through the start-up process and the operation of your business you will have many more opportunities to network. That means more opportunities to meet people who can direct you to work. A great way to meet influencers in the business world is to join the Chamber of Commerce serving your locality.

You will be joining as a small business owner, but your goal is to use the Chamber of Commerce to network with other business owners who may want to hire you or your small business. The Chamber of Commerce will hold many events designed to allow you to meet these people.

Note: Even if you are not starting your own business joining a chamber of commerce is a great way to meet business owners face to face. As a job seeker you work very hard to get you and your resume in front of the right decision maker.

Many chambers offer deeply discounted memberships to both unemployed and retired workers. For example, in Cranberry Township, Pennsylvania, the local chamber of commerce offers a $75.00 membership for those who are unemployed. This membership allows you to attend all of the chamber's networking breakfasts, lunches, and meetings each month. It is an excellent way to meet the owners and senior managers of many local companies.

The giant wart on your resume's beautiful face.

An employment gap can often be a flag on a resume suggesting to a hiring manager there was a problem; a problem she doesn't want to bring into her organization. That is why many job seekers are asked for more information about employment gaps during an interview.

The best way to handle doubts about employment gaps is to not list them. Have something else to put on your resume. This is where your small business comes in. Give yourself a job title and describe what it is you've been doing. Say you've been buying and reselling vintage baseball cards online and at weekend sports shows. You've been a "Salesman", "Buyer", or "Marketer", for example. You wouldn't explain your employment gap by saying you've simply been sitting in your house collecting unemployment for the last 4 months. You have been serving as the marketing coordinator for Sports Memorabilia Company.

Telling others what to do can pay very well.

Being a consultant is perhaps the easiest business to set up because the product is your expertise. You will get all the same advantages we've already discussed such as tax benefits, business experience, meeting new people, and eliminating a gap in your work history, but there is relatively little expense.

Additionally, every job you get hired to do as a consultant is basically a job interview on a grand scale. It is not uncommon for a company to offer consultants steady work for longer periods of time or even full-time employment.

Collecting unemployment while starting a business.

One important note to make is that in some states, such as Pennsylvania, you generally can't collect unemployment benefits if you are self-employed. If you tell the unemployment office you own your own business you will be denied benefits. There is an exception to that rule, however.

In Pennsylvania, for example, you can still collect your unemployment benefits if you meet these four criteria:

1. Concurrency - your self-employment activities must have been conducted while engaged in employment.

2. Primary Source of Income - the earnings from employment must exceed the net profit from the self-employment activities.

3. There cannot be a substantial increase in involvement in self-employment.

4. You are able and available for FULL TIME suitable work.

Remember, unless you are participating in the Self-Employment Assistance Program, the money you earn from your part-time small business must be claimed as income when you file your unemployment claim.

Self-employment Assistance Program (SEA).

The North American Free Trade Agreement (NAFTA) gave states the option of permitting unemployed individuals the ability to collect unemployment while working to become self-employed.

Your unemployment office can tell you if you are eligible to participate in the program. The unemployment office will determine your eligibility with these factors: you want to be self-employed, you are eligible for unemployment compensation and likely to exhaust your regular UC benefits, and you are able to satisfy any other requirements your particular locality may have.

The primary benefit to you, if you have lost your job and want to start a business, is that you can still collect the same amount of unemployment compensation and be excused from the requirement of actively searching for suitable work with an employer. This allows you to focus on building your business.

Additionally, the program is designed to offer training and counseling for new entrepreneurs. That means a counselor will be available to help you with such things as writing a business plan, getting loans, and marketing your business.

Believing in yourself.

Do you think you can't be a small business owner? Many very successful entrepreneurs started out as enthusiastic hobbyists with meager resources. As a young adult Henry Ford was working at a company owned by Thomas Edison and was making a modest salary of $45.00 per month. After coming home from his day job, he would work late into the night in his garage workshop constructing engines and mock cars. With only handmade tools, discarded spare parts, and scrap metal, he turned his interest in machinery into an incredibly successful venture.

How much money does it take to get started?

Of course, money is a key factor in starting a business, but it is far from the only factor. Not sure you have enough money to start your own business? Consider Paula Deen's story.

Paula Deen's start up story.

In May 2010, Paula Deen was on the Suze Orman show and an interesting fact about her business came up. Years ago, before Paula Deen became the successful entrepreneur that she is today, she was nearly destitute. Suze brought up the fact that Paula had started out with only $200.00, which immediately leads people interested in small business success stories to go learn more about how she did it. Paula Deen's biography is a great place to start.

Paula gives readers an honest and insightful look at her life in her book, "It Ain't All About Cookin'", from childhood to the incredible business success she is today. For those with an entrepreneur's heart you won't be able to put her book down.

If you are looking for inspiration while working on your own small business venture, Paula's story can be very motivating. Before Paula Deen was a business owner she was an employee. She held jobs such as a bank teller; a place where she was robbed at gun point. One job she was not at all proud of was when she accepted a job at Kroger grocery store, but couldn't even be a cashier; she had to start with the lowest paying cleaning job. However, at that point in her life she didn't have a choice, but to take whatever job she could get. More than once her family was faced with foreclosure and terrible financial crises.

Paula had a tremendous skill: cooking. Like for many small business owners, that skill was something that was marketable, even if she didn't fully recognize it at the time. Even though she didn't have experience in running a business, she had many other things that formed the foundation of her success: excellence at her craft, deathly determination, a strong work ethic, personality, and really no other choice but to succeed.

Paula used all the money she had, $200.00, and bought enough food and supplies to make about 40 tuna sandwiches and sell them in an office building during lunch time. She sold them all and her business, The Bag Lady, was born.

Paula went on to open a small catering business, open the Lady and Sons restaurant in Savannah, buy real estate, publish many recipe books, sell products on QVC, start a television show on the Food Network, star as a guest on Oprah, and even work with former President Jimmy Carter! Listed below you will find many of the key points and examples that were instrumental in Paula Deen's business success.

Business start-up tips from Paula Deen's story.

1. You have to work harder. Harder than what anyone else defines as "hard work". Paula even starts her book by mentioning that success only comes with hard work. You will never stop working. While luck can sometimes play a small part in success, Paula makes a great point. Luck sure seems to happen a lot more often when you are working extremely hard. Hard work builds positive forward momentum by creating an environment where tomorrow's greater accomplishments are made possible because of today's work.

2. Keep your costs low, especially during the fragile start up time. Paula had two excellent examples in "It Ain't All About Cookin'". When she starting out making lunches in her kitchen, she and those helping her, used (clean) underwear as hair nets, thus saving that cost! Additionally, she kept her living expenses very low, keeping the focus on business needs, rather than personal desires.

3. Your focus must be the business. Everything else is just background noise. Paula even mentioned that when major news stories were being reported she barely noticed. Her focus on building her business kept her from following stories like the O.J. Simpson trial, the Unabomber, or even the Oklahoma City Federal

Building bombing. If you're business is going to succeed, it must be the focus of all your effort and energy.

4. Quality and the customer's experience. Being the best in your niche and providing a quality product brings customers to your door. Paula had no money for advertising, but her welcoming personality and the notable quality of her meals led customers to tell others. Customers felt good about Paula; she has an inclusive personality that draws others in. Additionally, the quality of her cooking stood out and separated her from others. That word of mouth advertising was invaluable in getting Paula's catering and restaurant businesses off the ground.

Not sure how to get started? Here are 10 steps.

Write a basic business plan and answer these questions:

-Can I demonstrate that I am trying to make a profit?

   Very important!

-What product / service / or idea am I selling?

-Who is going to buy what I am selling?

   Who are my potential customers?

-Why would those potential customers buy from me?

   What makes me different?

-When will I sell my product / service / or idea?

   Seasonally? Once a year? Every day?

-How do I find my potential customers?

Decide on what your business name will be.

If you have chosen to not use your last name in your business name you must file with the state and list your fictitious name in the legal notices of a newspaper in the county in which your business will be based.

Create a filing and recordkeeping system.

In addition to records of your personal expenditures, every expense you incur, in which your small business had some part of, should be documented. Also document business transactions such as applying for licenses or permits. Keep the paperwork from everything. You and your accountant will be very glad you did this when it comes time to do your taxes!

Your filing system can contain these categories: Marketing, Advertising, Operations, Taxes, Legal, and Sales.

-Taxes – any documents in regard to taxes owed or paid

-Legal – documents such as permits, licenses, and your EIN number

-Advertising – documents regarding the actual advertisements you do and their expense

-Sales – documents regarding the activities you do and the expenses you incur in order to make the actual sale such as training, classes, and education materials. Additionally, what this step means to you is that you must carefully and accurately record any income you make from your small business. You will need that information so your accountant can properly complete your tax return.

-*Marketing* – documents regarding the activities you do and the expenses you incur in order to draw in customers – such as a website

-*Operations* – documents regarding the activities you do and the expenses you incur in order to prepare and deliver your products – such as materials to build it

*Apply for an Employer Identification Number from the IRS

You may want to do this even if you will not be hiring anyone. That is because many banks will only allow you to open a business checking account if you have an EIN number.

*Apply for a sales tax identification number

You will go through this step only if you are not going to form a sole proprietorship. You can generally do this online through your state's website.

*Apply for an operating or occupancy permit through the municipality if it is required.

Do this through the municipality building in the area in which you plan to base your small business.

*Open a checking account at your bank under your business name.

The IRS loves to see you keep your small business income separate from your personal income from a job. This will not affect your ability to take tax deductions. You will need your EIN number and driver's license to open that account.

Work with a counselor who can walk you through any questions.

Save yourself time and expense by working with someone who has gone through this before. This should be someone that can point out additional opportunities to take tax deductions and walk you through things like marketing, advertising, and operations when you are ready to start selling.

Additionally, if you ever need to hire someone, either an employee or contractor, don't settle for anything less than excellent performance. Receiving less than excellent performance from paid labor will kill your small business.

Look for tax deductions.

Question every penny you spend. Ask yourself – does this / can this expenditure have a business purpose? Can it be tax deductible?

Start selling!

Go make some money!

Key Takeaway: going through the motions of starting your own business provides you a lot of relevant experience, connections, and practice that is transferrable to both a new job and a second income.

How Much Is Your Education Worth

"I have to do something with my mind, or I'll get in trouble." Vince McMahon, owner of WWE

If you do not have a high school diploma you should make it a priority to obtain a GED during this time. There are many reasons why you should invest in education, but your income potential is the most important one. Consider this excerpt from a recent article in *The Quarter Roll*.

While there has been some debate on what the Pittsburgh School District's high school graduation rate is, several studies put it under 70%. Pennsylvania's average is 78%.

That means that nearly a third of Pittsburgh high school kids will enter the workforce at a distinct disadvantage at a time when the economy has been particularly harsh on non-graduates. One's level of education does make a difference in someone's ability to earn higher levels of income and even get hired.

Salary expectations by education level.

The average salary someone can expect to earn without a high school education is $21,000.00 per year, compared to a high school graduate who makes 50% more at $31,000.00 per year.

Knowing about the potential 50% jump in pay may be an incentive to get many kids to complete their studies and graduate from high school. Education is not the only thing that will allow someone to earn more at work, but it certainly proves to be a major factor.

Unemployment rate by education level.

However, when you dig into the average unemployment rate and consider education level you find even worse news for those

without a high school diploma. These seasonally adjusted numbers are listed as of July 2011:
Unemployment rate for those with no high school diploma: 15%
Unemployment rate for those with a high school diploma: 9.3%
Unemployment rate for those with some college: 8.3%
Unemployment rate for those with a college diploma: 4.3%

Career training.

Education doesn't just include high school and college studies. If you had your last job for a long period of time you may not have much experience in career planning, networking, or scouting for work and interviewing. The good news is that there is lots of free, professional help to educate you how to quickly get a new job and it's probably much closer to your home than you think.

Check out the career services that libraries around your home may offer. The Cuyahoga County Public Library in Parma, Ohio, for example, says that their career counselors assist members of the community with career planning, targeting companies and jobs that are in demand, creating resumes & cover letters, and preparing for a job interview. Additionally, their counselors provide free training classes with titles such as:

-Career Planning

-Creating Cover Letters

-Effective Networking

-Internet Job Search

-LinkedIn 101

-Online Job Applications

-Over 50 & Out of Work

-Resumes Tips & Trends

-Social Networking & Your Job Search

-Steps to Effective Interviewing

-Targeting Companies for Your Job Search

How NOT To Pay For College

A common topic that comes up when people lose their job is retraining or taking additional classes that could enhance one's work skills. There are many reasons why this is a great idea. As you will discover, one of the "silver linings" in unemployment is the number of options you will have available to you in order to further your education and improve your own personal marketability when seeking a new job.

Going to school while unemployed also helps you maintain your professional focus. We are not talking about taking clay pottery or swimming classes (unless those happen to be your profession). The education you are seeking is such that will bring your skills or credentials up to date, or provide you with additional knowledge that allows you to qualify for even more jobs in your chosen industry.

Even on the basic level of following a schedule, completing assignments, and solving industry related problems in class you are keeping your focus sharp. It could allow you to meet people in your field who can recommend you to employers. At an interview, it could even help you sound like someone who is still very active in the industry versus someone who has been lounging for months.

111

Many people express a desire to go back to school and finish a degree or earn a professional designation. Of course two major obstacles many people run into are time and money. Certainly, at this point you should have some more time. Just by eliminating your commute you have freed up time that can be applied toward further education. You will also see that the second obstacle, money, isn't as large a problem as you may have thought.

We will investigate many options available to you that can dramatically reduce the cost of your education. While there are a multitude of options that can help you pay for your continued education, many programs will not cover the entire amount as college costs can be quite high. However, you will see that it is possible to create a strategic plan where you combine several programs which can lead to an entirely free education.

Don't get the wrong idea. You are not about to get the secret location of the generous philanthropist who hands over $20,000.00 checks to each student that finds him. You will need to have a degree of flexibility. Keep in mind that during this time in your life preserving your assets and cash is of critical importance.

At the same time though, molding yourself into the most ideal job candidate could mean additional financial costs. Even the IRS realizes it can cost money to find a new job, and offers special tax deductions to active job seekers. You shouldn't consider personal or student loans for a number of reasons, one of which is that there are a variety of funding alternatives available.

Ask a professional.

Assuming you have a general idea of the educational programs you are interested in and would make you a more attractive job candidate, your first visit should be the financial aid office of your first two or three school choices. Stop in on a Tuesday, Wednesday, or Thursday when the office is typically slower.

Ideally, you will be able to visit during a week other than the first couple of week before classes start or during a holiday. The reason for timing your visit like this is you want to be sure a school representative will have more time to spend with you individually, listen to your specific goals, and review all the options available.

The reason why you want to visit a financial aid representative at their school's home office is that these professionals make a living out of finding money earmarked for education. If you want arteries unclogged you go to a doctor, if you want the waist of your pants brought in you go to tailor, and if you want money for education you need to go see the financial aid professionals!

These folks are eager to help you pay for your educational goals. Further, by explaining in detail what you need to accomplish and why, they will be able to hone in on specific programs that can financially support your goals.

Be sure to visit more than one financial aid office. Any advisor who is willing to share her insights with you regarding tuition assistance will prove invaluable. However, some schools specialize in particular courses of study and focus primarily on programs available for those classes. By interviewing 2 or 3 advisors from different schools you may gain additional knowledge about less advertised niche programs other schools have not worked with before.

Visiting in person is better than asking questions on the phone, because the advisor may be able to suggest additional people you can visit for advice while you are there. Also, you will find that people are more willing to help you, when you've demonstrated your serious intent to pursue education by physically showing up at their door.

Federal grants.

Keeping in mind that cash and asset preservation should be a priority of yours, you will want to collect education funding that comes with no repayment strings attached. You are looking for money in the form of grants. Grants will typically have requirements that must be met in order be awarded the money.

Our "Uncle Sam" is one place you can find an educational grant with no repayment obligation. The website studentaid.ed.gov states, "The Free Application for Federal Student Aid (FAFSA) is the form used by virtually all two and four-year colleges, universities and career schools for the awarding of federal student aid and most state and college aid."

As with most grants, the federal money available for education has an eligibility requirement based on income. The application process includes a very thorough review of your financial standing, including the amount of cash and assets you have. Your assets are part of the equation in determining your eligibility.

As of 2011 the maximum award through the Federal Pell Grant program is $5,550.00. A determination of your household's financial strength will determine the amount you are awarded. Application does not guarantee an award, but everyone is welcome and encouraged to apply. According to ThePellGrant.com, "Students with a total family income up to $50,000 may be eligible for Pell Grants, though most Pell funding goes to students with a total family income below $20,000."

State grants.

Details and benefits through state educational grants may vary, so be sure to ask about the specifics of your state's program when visiting the financial aid offices. The Pennsylvania Higher Education Assistance Agency (PHEAA) is Pennsylvania's resource for applying for state aid. Some requirements for Pennsylvania student grants include not having previously earned a bachelor's degree or its equivalent, you need to be a graduate of an approved high school or have a GED, you have to attend a PHEAA-approved school, and you must meet criteria for financial need.

Just like the application for federal student aid, your state will want to review your personal financial standing and assess your ability to pay based on your net assets. However, just like federal aid, you have nothing to lose and everything to gain by completing the application process. After all, you are filling out an application for free money!

The PHEAA website states as of 2011, "While the current formula provides for awards up to $4,700 while attending an approved Pennsylvania institution, currently the State Grant Program does not have sufficient resources to fully fund this amount. Therefore, adjustments to bring awards within the funding level are necessary. (Note: Annually, the maximum award is dependent on available funding and subject to review and adjustment.)"

Unemployment benefits.

Most people are aware that there are programs available through state unemployment agencies, which assist dislocated workers with enhancing their work skills through training and education. However, many people are not fully aware of the requirements, benefits, or limitations of this training. Understanding how the system works will allow you to maximize this incredible benefit.

Tuition assistance through the unemployment agency is for dislocated workers. A dislocated worker is someone who lost their job involuntary and through no fault of their own. If you were fired from your job for fighting a co-worker, you are not a dislocated worker, and will not be eligible for any of these benefits.

Education and training benefits will be available to you in addition to your unemployment benefit. Unlike the money amount you will receive to replace your job income, the education benefit is not based on the amount of money you were making. The money you receive does not have to be used strictly on tuition. For example, it can be used for school related costs such as required books, fees, study materials, and calculators.

The amount of assistance you receive will first be based on the amount the particular county you reside in has available. In Pennsylvania not all counties pay dislocated workers the same amount. For example, in February 2011 the cap for tuition assistance in Allegheny County was $8,000.00, while the cap in Westmoreland County was several thousand dollars less.

This benefit is provided so that you can enhance your job skills and get an equivalent or better position. That means you must study something related to the industry you were working in. So if you were designing computer systems, you will not be awarded money to learn how to play the guitar. An exception to this requirement is training that would prepare you for "in demand" jobs. Your unemployment agency will have a list of these "in demand" occupations.

The list of college courses eligible for this program has been expanded. Talking to a representative at the unemployment office will give you the most up to date information that is available. You may not have thought a program at prestigious Duquesne University in Pittsburgh would be eligible for tuition reimbursement, but their Executive Certificate in Financial Planning course is. This is an excellent example of a program that is not a degree program, but will give someone skills that are in high demand and command excellent salaries.

Even if you are not interested in obtaining a college degree, you should think very hard before passing up this opportunity. Generally speaking, the total amount you qualify for may not cover the entire cost of a particular program, but there are many programs you can choose from. Use the benefit and go learn something new that will help you obtain higher paying employment.

Community college for dislocated workers.

The Community College of Allegheny County is a good representation of many community colleges across our nation that offer specialized programs to assist dislocated workers get a degree. The Dislocated Worker Tuition Waiver program is one such example.

According to the CCAC website: "Dislocated workers may take classes at CCAC toward the successful completion of one of the approved certificate programs for free tuition and fees only (no more than 36 credits within a 24-month period)."

In this program you must apply for financial aid in the form of grants; you are not required to explore loan options. The amount not covered by any grants you qualify for will be paid for through this program. Remember though that tuition is only paid for study in fields that are deemed high demand or high priority. The college's financial aid department would be able to provide you with that list.

Employers who pay your tuition.

In Chapter 3 we discussed the benefits of taking a part-time job. The unemployment office can tell you how much you can earn before you start to see a reduction in the dollar benefit you are entitled to. With a part-time job and the unemployment benefit you could be earning nearly as much as you did from your full-time job.

If you are searching for a part-time job, be sure to look for additional benefits that will assist you in being more marketable. First, take a part-time job that will teach you something new that you can leverage into a better paying job. Secondly, take a job with a company that offers tuition reimbursement to part-time employees.

Many local companies in Pittsburgh, for example, offer tuition repayment to both full and part-time employees. Some of those companies include Huntington Bank, PNC, UPMC, Dollar Bank, Heinz, Allegheny Financial and Verizon.

As of 2010, the IRS said that employees can receive as much as $5,250.00for graduate or undergraduate tuition, fees, books and supplies before that benefit is included in the employee's gross taxable income. That means if you found an employer who gave you $6,000 toward your education expenses you would have to pay tax on $750.00 of it.

Most companies will list the fringe benefits they offer on the "Careers" page of their websites. When considering a part-time position with a particular company, be sure to visit that page. You can also actively seek out companies with this benefit and approach them for part-time work rather than waiting for a job listing to be posted.

How volunteering can pay for college.

Like many community colleges, the Community College of Allegheny County offers an incredible free tuition incentive for volunteer firefighters. Many community colleges are doing this as well, and some states include EMTs, full time firefighters, and rescue squad workers.

Most volunteer fire fighting stations will tell you their two primary struggles are raising money for appropriate equipment and attracting enough volunteers. According to the National Fire Protection Association over 50% of all volunteer firefighters are over the age of 40. In an effort to entice younger community members to volunteer many community colleges offer free tuition as an enticement.

In the CCAC example above, some of the conditions to receiving the free tuition are that the volunteer serves for at least 5 years, complete the free fire fighting training courses, and maintain at least a 2.0 grade point average. Unlike some other tuition assistance programs, there are no restrictions on what you can study.

Using some of your time, while searching for a new job, to train for work at your local volunteer fire fighting station can provide you tuition assistance, networking opportunities, and resume building experience.

Key Takeaway: How do you earn free tuition, serve your community, learn new skills, and fill an employment gap? Become a volunteer firefighter.

Combine study and work.

Nearly all colleges and universities offer free, or dramatically discounted tuition, to their employees, and often to the employees' family members as well.

Just like many other organizations, colleges will list campus jobs on their website. Colleges hire both full and part-time help. For example, Duquesne University offers 100% tuition remission for full-time employees and 50% tuition remission for part-time employees. Not sure if that is a good benefit? Consider this. The average tuition cost for 2 semesters at Duquesne University is $31,553.00 (without room and board). As a part-time employee you are entitled to a 50% tuition reduction, or in this case, $15,776.00!

Serving in the military.

The military has long touted its' educational and career building benefits. Generally, people are familiar with the fact that the military offers paid training in 150+ military specialties, and most of those skills are transferable to civilian careers. Additionally, it is a well-known fact that the military offers scholarship money to active members and veterans. However, a lesser known fact is the variety of ways an individual can serve in the military and still enjoy the generous educational benefits only the United States military can offer.

For the purposes of this book, there are two primary reasons why someone under the age of 40 may want to consider military service if they have lost their job. The first is that the military is hiring for both full and part-time positions right now, and even the lowest ranking recruit receives pay, health insurance, fringe benefits, training, and educational assistance. Secondly, even for part-time reservists, there are a number of tuition assistance and repayment programs available.

Every branch of the armed services has aptitude tests (known as the Armed Services Vocational Aptitude Battery) and physical fitness requirements one much meet in order to enlist. However, once you pass these requirements you can be working within a very short period of time.

In 2010 the average length of time on unemployment was 35 weeks. That means a gap in your employment history and a reduction in your household income for well over a half year. Why not fill that time with military employment?

Basic training is typically 9 weeks and advanced skills training can range from 12 to 52 weeks, depending on the military specialty you have opted for. As a reservist, once your initial training is completed you will return home with a regular part-time job, excellent benefits, marketable new skills and experience, and access to the military's tuition assistance programs.

The Army, for example, offers two tuition assistance programs: The Montgomery GI Bill (MGIB) and the Army College Fund (ACF). All soldiers can participate in the MGIB, and the ACF can be combined with it in order to further increase the amount of benefit. The tuition benefit for reservists is lower than for those who served full-time. For example, an active duty soldier who served for two years, and contributed $1,200.00 into the Montgomery GI Bill, would be eligible for $1,158.00 per month for 36 months, or $41,688.00, while in college after the enlistment was completed. A reservist would be eligible for about $340.00 per month.

The Army College Fund is only available to full-time soldiers who score 50 or higher on the Armed Services Vocational Aptitude Battery test and are serving in selected military occupations that have a shortage of personnel. That list of occupations changes regularly, but an Army recruiter would be able to provide a current list. These benefits can be used for associates, bachelors, graduate, doctorate, or professional degrees.

According to the Department of Veteran Affairs, "Some reservists may contribute up to an additional $600 to the GI Bill to receive increased monthly benefits. For an additional $600 contribution, you may receive up to $5400 in additional GI Bill benefits. You must be a member of a Ready Reserve component (Selected Reserve, Individual Ready Reserve, or Inactive National Guard) to pay into the "buy-up" program."

The Army also offers tuition assistance to both Army and Army Reserve soldiers during their enlistments. The Army and Army Reserve will fund 100% of course costs up to $250.00 per credit hour, with a maximum of $4,500.00 per academic year.

Military service can be a fresh career start. Military experience is an attractive addition to any resume. Few organizations provide paid training in high demand occupations while giving you a paycheck. Already have a college degree? The military offers opportunities for college graduates to join at higher paid ranks.

What if you have a bachelor's degree and the student loans that came with it? The military can help you with that as well. As a reservist you could be qualified for up to $40,000.00 in student loan repayment assistance. This amount is not given in one lump sum, but over time while you are in the service.

Concerned that you may be recalled back to work while you are training with the military? Don't let that stop you from enlisting. In a case where you are subject to be recalled to work because you were laid off due to a work shortage, and your position was not eliminated, you are covered under The Uniformed Services Employment and Reemployment Rights Act of 1994.

This law protects you from losing any seniority, pay, or benefits you may have been entitled to, even if you were not enlisting in the military or leaving to fulfill training or service requirements.

One important thing to remember about enlisting in the military, especially considering the state many countries find themselves in, is that active duty deployment is almost guaranteed at some point whether you are enrolled as an active duty soldier or in the reserves.

Key Takeaway: Consider military service. In the average length of time a dislocated worker spends on unemployment, he or she could become a military reservist, entitled to pay, insurance, advanced training, and generous assistance with the cost of further education.

Chapter 5

Finding work

Chapter Overview

In her book *Bait and Switch*, Barbara Ehrenreich tells of her experiment in going "undercover" as a recently unemployed professional looking for a new job. Throughout the book she details the number of career coaches, networking events, and workshops she visited. Even with her honest attempts in doing all of the exercises and tasks she was assigned, she did not come up with a new job.

Many of the groups she attended wanted a fee for participation or had other goals besides business networking. For example, many of the church based unemployment support meetings she went to were more focused on prayer and Biblical lessons.

Thought staying at home and using the web was a more efficient way of finding a job? A story on CNNMoney.com made the point that a pathetic 4% of open positions were filled by referrals from CareerBuilder.com, a major player in the job website business.

Rather than pay someone else or depend on volunteers to help you find a job, create a game plan on your own, using your own network of resources and contacts. Career coach Dan Miller says, "Network constantly. Start each day with an action plan. Get out there and meet people. Talk to anyone you can who might offer suggestions on how to improve your job search. Don't be embarrassed to let people know you are looking for work. You are selling a product, and that product is YOU."

Today, the web can be your most powerful ally, but it can also be a crutch that keeps you paralyzed in inaction, glued to the front of a computer screen. Secondly, old fashion sales techniques will break the ice in getting you in front of the right people who will hire you.

Where To Look For Jobs

If you could work for any company, where would you work? Now, ask yourself why you would want to work for them. Is it because of their reputation for employee benefits, their unique products or services, or the industry they are in? What other companies closely match the values of the one you have in mind? Make a long list of employers you want to work for or may want to work for.

Research these companies and learn everything you can about them. Most importantly, however, search their website for jobs. For a variety of reasons, many companies do not pay to advertise any (or some) of their open positions. Rather, they list them on their own website. Visit the career pages of the companies you would like to work for in addition to your other job hunting activities.

Key Takeaway: Many jobs are not advertised in the newspaper or online job boards. So go right to the source of the jobs: the companies themselves.

Specific company websites.

When you have a list of companies you would like to work for, visit their website and search the job openings. You may find many of the job opportunities you find on their own website were not advertised elsewhere.

A tool for helping facilitate this type of search is LinkUp.com. LinkUp.com is a job search engine that only lists jobs found on company websites. This makes it much easier to quickly find unadvertised positions.

LinkUp.com does not search other job boards in order to collect job postings for its' own site, and LinkUp.com doesn't currently allow employers to list open positions on their site. LinkUp.com's website claims to have over 700,000 jobs listed from 21,000+ employer websites.

Why you should attend job fairs.

"When you meet someone face-to-face, you might not know exactly how old they are. But online you might develop these stringent criteria, like 'If you're 35, I'll date you, but if you're 36, forget it.'" (Jennifer Gibbs, communications assistant professor at Rutgers, explains how dating-related "flaws" seem relatively minor offline become magnified online. Source: Discovery News via Smart Computing April 2011)

Job fairs are appealing for a number of reasons, but the best one of all may be the fact that you are physically in front of an employer. Resumes on fancy paper just don't cut it anymore. There are too many of them, and honestly, after the first 20 or 30 of them your eyes start to glaze over from the sameness of them all.

Consider the three primary ways people learn:

Visual style – learning by seeing (60% of us)

Auditory style – learning by hearing (30% of us)

Kinesthetic style – learning by touching or moving (10% of us)

For a person who learns visually, this means you will struggle to keep her attention if she can't see you. She may "hear" you, but she may not be listening. Imagine how a phone interview goes if you are talking to a hiring manager who is a visual learner. They may not hear a thing you say.

At a job fair you have the opportunity to keep the attention of someone regardless of their learning style.

How will you know which learning style to appeal to? Just pay attention to the interviewer for clues. For example, if she appears to be looking you and the room over for details, point things out for her to look at, such as the various supporting documents you have with you. Auditory learners speak with and listen for variation in tones and enunciation. If she seems to touch things or move around more often, mimic her behavior; move your things or resume around the desk and "talk" with your hands.

Key Takeaway: Standing in front of employers at a job fair allows you to connect with them using all three of the learning methods.

It also means your best representative, YOU, not your resume, is speaking on your behalf.

The good, the bad, and the ugly when it comes to job fairs.

The good.

The good is that you meet face to face. The worst way to get a job is to send someone a resume. Your piece of paper, regardless of the font, keywords, or the weight of the paper you use, is just another piece of paper; most likely to be scanned by a machine or reviewed by an overworked and uncaring human resources assistant. YOU are what managers need to see, not just your credentials. You can't do that without a face to face meeting.

Job fairs are where hiring managers finally come out from behind their access controlled corporate offices and greet the job seeking public.

The bad.

The bad is somewhat related to the good in that this isn't as much an interview as it is a quick meeting to size you up. In some cases you will only have a minute or two in order to make a good impression on the company. You need to have dressed appropriately for the type of jobs offered at this job fair, quickly build a rapport with the hiring manager, effectively sell 2 or 3 key points why you are an ideal candidate, and have a well written resume to leave.

Not sure how to build rapport in under 60 seconds? Using internet access from your phone or the facility at which the job fair is being held, look up news about the company from this week.

For example, you discover that Company A just received the Community Citizen award at a dinner held last night. You approach the company's booth and say "Good morning! My name is Joe Smith. Congratulations on receiving the Community Citizen award last night!". 1) You've broken the ice by giving the company representative an easy topic with which to start talking to you about, and 2) you are standing out from all the other candidates who didn't know about the Community Citizen award.

Key Takeaway: At a job fair you may only have the hiring manager's attention for one minute. Use that minute wisely. Plan ahead and have something interesting to bring up that is both timely and relevant.

The ugly.

Believe it or not there can be two somewhat ugly elements to a job fair. The first can be the company representatives themselves, who rarely get out or are usually not asked to do any out of the ordinary assignments. However, today they were asked to staff the company's booth at the job fair.

These guys are easily identified by their excessive giddiness for being allowed out of the office for a day, having the company buy them a lunchtime sandwich, and wielding some sort of perceived power over your future with the company. They may look pathetic, but if you are convinced you want to work for the company you can still leave your resume to be turned over to their human resources department.

Secondly, look out for the job seekers whose anxious appearance is fueled by desperation. They are going to try and edge anyone else out by monopolizing as much of a hiring manager's time as possible, thus leaving less time for you to get your face time. Ultimately, this strategy backfires on them as no company wants to spend more than a few minutes with each candidate.

Don't spend an excessive amount of time waiting behind a line of talkers. You can come back to this booth later. Go visit other booths, even if you don't think they have a job you are interested in, rather than just standing in line. Visiting all the booths at the job fair may let you discover unrealized job opportunities or meet a new contact.

Job fairs: why businesses attend and you should too.

Many companies will advertise the positions they are seeking to fill prior to the job fair they will be attending. However, even if you don't see a job you are interested in, or qualified for, you should use this opportunity to meet the hiring managers for the companies in attendance. There are several reasons why.

First, meeting an insider at that company will give you an opportunity to pitch your resume and perhaps see where else you might fit into their organization. This is especially helpful if that particular company is on your list of targeted businesses for who you would like to work.

A job seeker's version of speed dating.

A second reason to attend is to get a lot of practice interviewing. Ever hear of "speed dating"? This is an event where a large group of single people meet each other one and one for only a few minutes. In that few minutes they have an opportunity to learn about each other and pitch the reasons why they would make a good date.

Much like speed dating, job fair interviews are short and specific. That means you have to be comfortable giving your own interview version of an elevator speech. Doing this with 10-15 interviewers in one day versus 30 days will quickly allow you to polish your presentation.

Finally, human resource professionals and their staff of interviewers are some of the best connected people in business. Just like a salesman, who didn't make a sale, knows to ask for references of people who would be interested in what she is selling, you should ask the interviewer if she knows another employer who would be interested in your experience. If you are referred to someone else be sure to mention the name of the person who referred you when you meet the other employer!

Once you've met these company representatives be sure to get their business cards. That will give you key contact information should you need it now to follow up on a conversation you had or in the future when you find other job openings at that company. On the back of the card write down something about that person that will help you remember them in more detail.

How to find job fairs.

Where do you look for job fairs close to your home? There are plenty of resources online that offer databases and calendars listing job fairs across the country on any particular date. Try employmentguide.com, nationalcareerfairs.com, or coasttocoastcareerfairs.com.

What employers are doing at job fairs.

For an employer a job fair is like the crab pots you see the fisherman using from "The Deadliest Catch" reality show. They can scoop up hundreds of crabs all at once, rather than just a few at a time. By the way, YOU are one of the crabs! How will you stand out from everyone else? Read Adam Kickish's job fair success story, and find out what his suggestion is.

Key Takeaway: The two best things you can use a job fair for as a job seeker is getting face time with a key contact person and using their time to hone your own interviewing and networking skills. Be positive, get to the point, and be prepared when you attend a job fair.

Adam Kickish's job fair success story.

Adam Kickish's career as a loss prevention and safety manager was unexpectedly derailed one afternoon when his boss called him into an office and informed him that he was being laid off. Adam was told that the lay-off had nothing to do with the quality of his work, but that the company was failing and could no longer afford him.

Adam soon found out that he was not the only person being let go that day, as he ran into many laid off employees from other departments making their way down hallways toward the front of the building.

Adam knew right away it was going to be difficult to quickly replace his salary and get his career back on track. However, he didn't let that challenge stop him from aggressively looking for work. Proving that persistence pays off, Adam had a new professional level job within 8 weeks of losing his last position. How did he do it?

During the time he was laid off, Adam tried many of the standard practices a job seeker would normally try. He searched job boards, contacted people in his professional network, and asked for referrals. However, Adam says that it was going to a job fair that made the difference.

When he went to the job fair Adam's expectations weren't high, as there was lots of competition, but he visited each employer's booth anyway. Adam said, "There were so many people there, and the employers at each booth had collections of resumes as thick as phone books." Adam had two personal goals for this job fair. First, he wanted to meet decision makers and get some kind of inside information about their company and them personally. That would be information he could use down the road if he applied for other jobs.

How Adam stood out.

"My other goal was to stand out from the rest of the group. I did that by mirroring the behavior of the company representative. If he was upbeat I was upbeat. If he was more laid back that is how I acted." At one booth Adam noted that they had no appropriate jobs listed for him, but he took the time to introduce himself anyway.

That hiring manager realized Adam was an ideal fit for another division of the company. That brief meeting led to two interviews and a job offer not long afterwards. Today, Adam is employed in a growing industry and his career is strongly moving forward.

Resumes and Interview Strategies

Direct mail and e-mail.

Many newspapers and business journals report the successes, failures, and current projects of companies. This type of media will give you a gold mine of information about how a particular company could use you. With that information you can contact the appropriate person via a letter or email and let them know how your work experience could solve their problem or enhance the value they want to achieve in a particular product. Your insight, solution, and initiative will attract positive attention.

Jacob was a customer service manager. He wanted to work for a nationally known mail order company. He searched news, complaint boards, and blogs about the company and discovered they had recently started a customer rewards program that was not working the way the company had intended. In fact there were many complaints about it online.

What Jacob realized though was that the company he was working for had gone through the same thing, and he had designed a solution that solved the problem and kept the expense to a minimum. He mailed a letter to the vice president in charge of sales, summarized the problem, and offered a solution. He didn't receive a response that first time, but he kept this practice up with multiple companies until he was eventually hired for his ideas and solutions.

Website resumes.

Another way of finding a job is to let the job find you. Today there are many mediums through which you can attract attention to yourself and the skills you have to offer an employer. Creating a digital resume is one sure way to stand out from the competition and at the same time, create a way for employers to discover you.

John Williams of Ann Arbor, Michigan, was one of thousands in the financial industry to lose his job during the recession. John realized obtaining a new job in the financial industry would be tough, but with a wife and 3 kids depending on him it was necessary to quickly find employment.

John had a lot working against him. Michigan's unemployment rate was one of the worst in the country, and competition for work was fierce. He needed a way to stand out.

It was this need to be different from all the other job candidates that led John to create his own website. Through Wordpress.com, he was able to buy a domain name and use pre-made templates to create a multipage site that would include his resume, accomplishments, interests, and a short biography. For well under $50.00 he launched HireJohnWilliams.com, and now had a tool that would help him reach employers in unique ways.

Why you should HireJohnWilliams.com.

This website gave John two advantages. The first was that, in addition to John searching for employers, companies looking for John's particular skills could also *find him* through an internet search.

When he first created the site John considered himself average when it came to technology. However, the site gave him was the appearance of a person with ultra-modern technological skills, something extra that would give him another marketable advantage when compared to other job candidates.

What should be on your website? John suggests that your site include your resume, of course. However, use this tool to demonstrate why you are different from other candidates and a better choice. John says on his site that he intends to give employers "...a better understanding of who I am as an individual and what I bring to the table as a potential employee."

John's advice to job seekers is to use a website as a tool with which to supplement your overall job hunting efforts. John stated in our interview, "You really need to get out there and find the places where business people are congregating and put yourself in front them". Your resume website will enhance your credibility and marketability when meeting and interacting with hiring managers.

Can your video camera help you get a job?

Perhaps a visual demonstration of your talent is more appropriate. YouTube gives employers a chance to see you in action. A video of you interacting with customers, selling something, speaking, or even juggling (if you are applying to the circus) will show employers you would be a great catch.

Don't think online resumes or YouTube videos are a serious way of finding work? Ask Justin Bieber about YouTube. Justin Bieber was in his very early teens when he and his mom posted videos of his singing on YouTube. This tremendously talented child singer was good enough to attract the attention of more than just friends and family.

Bieber said that at first there were a few hundred views, than a thousand, then ten thousand. His homemade singing videos started to pick up momentum and attracted the attention of industry megastars Usher and Justin Timberlake, both of whom started wooing Bieber to sign contracts with their own individual music production companies.

Unlike so many other child music stars Bieber did not have any real industry experience or inside contacts. He was a regular kid in a single parent home with a video camera.

Resumes of the future? The 1 page promotional advertisement.

Using keywords on your resume is important. It makes sense to customize your resume so that highlights skills you have that are highly relevant to the job you are applying for. The words you use, and how you write your resume, are important. However, remember that most people need to be visually stimulated in order to get and hold their attention.

We've talked about website resumes and video resumes, but you will often put a paper resume in someone's hands or an electronic resume in their inbox. Guess what all resumes look like after the 100th resume, no matter what keywords you have in it? A blob of colorless words on a white background. How do you make your resume stand out?

We mentioned that most of us are visual learners and that we are easily distracted by visually appealing things to look at. So, how do you keep a visual learner's attention on your resume?

Consider a resume that looks more like a promotional advertisement. In June 2011, Mashable.com ran the story "7 Ingenious Resumes That Will Make You Rethink Your CV". This article displayed some of the most unique ideas for creating a resume you will ever find. These resumes seemed to have morphed into visually exciting creations of sales art work.

Rather than looking like the traditionally structured resume, these resumes took the same information, broke the old rules, and pieced it all together in a one page poster like collage. Depending on the industry or position you are applying for, you can tell your story through a simple design all the way to splashes of color and pictures. An example is in the Resources chapter of this book.

Keeping in mind that not all industries, such as a conservative institution of higher learning, will appreciate this kind of creativity, the document you create will be a resume (or cover letter) that distinctly stands out from all others.

Be a problem solver.

Joe Turner, writing for Monster.com, suggested in his article, "Six Must-Ask Interview Questions", that during an interview you ask, "What is the first problem the person you hire must attend to?". This particular question reveals that you know why you are sitting in front of the hiring manager. You are there to explain how you can solve the company's problem. Problem solvers get jobs.

Many applicants take the wrong approach when reaching out to a company for a job. They can appear like beggars with their hands extended looking for charitable benevolence. These people will tell the company things like "I need a job." or "I want job security." or "I need the money." If you spent the last 10 years tucked away somewhere in a comfortable, quiet workspace this may sound shockingly cold to you, but guess what. Companies care a lot more about their own problems than yours!

What the company cares about.

The truth is the company doesn't care why you need a job. They advertised the job because they have a need or problem. They are looking for a solution. What is another reason so many resumes look the same? They are missing a key element. They don't clearly articulate how the applicant can solve a problem or immediately add value to the hiring company.

Yes, a resume should tell the company about you, but how you present it should clearly demonstrate your familiarity with the company's problems, needs, or goals and the solution you have to offer.

Have you ever heard the sales adage people don't buy cars, they buy transportation? Customers don't buy clothes, they buy fashion. They don't pay tuition for an education; they are investing in better wages sometime in the future. The same is true with employers. They aren't hiring just to do a good deed and give someone a job; they are hiring a solution to their problem. Remember, you aren't just asking for a job, you are offering a solution.

Offering solutions.

How do you find out what their needs or problems are? One way is to tune into the buzz online and hear what the company's customers are saying. Bonnie was a customer service manager who wanted to work for national floral and gift company. She was granted a phone interview, but knew that in order to attract a second look and job offer she would need to demonstrate she could add value and solve problems for the company.

Before her phone interview, Bonnie got on the web and discovered that several of the company's customers had registered complaints on consumer websites about a new rewards program the company was offering. It turned out that these problems were nearly identical to the problems Bonnie's employer had gone through about a year ago.

During her phone interview Bonnie was asked what she knew about the company. She mentioned the problem that was occurring. The interviewer was a little surprised to hear that someone outside of the company was so versed on what was going on. (The interviewer hadn't checked the complaint sites.) Bonnie further went on to offer several possible courses of action that could solve the problem. The interviewer was impressed and asked Bonnie to come in and discuss her solutions with the senior managers, thus putting her directly in front of the ultimate decision makers.

Talk to this angry customer for me.

Sometimes you may not see the pressing need of the company until you are standing right in the middle of it. When I interviewed for my customer service position at Roomful Express Furniture, the boss's phone was ringing non-stop. He explained that since there was currently no customer service manager he was getting all the escalated problem calls.

I seized the opportunity to suggest I would be able to solve that problem for him immediately as I had been working in customer service for years. He took me up on the offer and suggested I go ahead and answer his phone the next time it rang. When it rang, I answered the phone and identified myself as someone from the company's customer service department. As the hiring manager looked on, I took the customer's complaint, empathized with the customer's plight, and promised his concerns would be investigated and he would receive a call back. The customer had calmed down and I was hired.

Who are the best references?

Hiring managers who have been interviewing for any length of time know that generally speaking, applicants are going to coach the references they list on their resume. The game goes like this. I tell the hiring manager you can call my associate George Washington for a reference, but we both know I called George last night and coached him on what I would like him to say if he is called. Secondly, hiring managers know that the people who have nothing good to say about you won't take their calls. They are afraid of saying the wrong thing and being sued.

Meaningful references can play a significant role in getting a job offer though. The catch? The reference you give must be meaningful to the hiring manager. The best references you can have are from people the hiring manager knows, respects, or works with.

Ever hear of the "6 degrees of separation" theory? This theory says everyone is approximately six steps away from being connected to any other person on Earth. Your job is find the links (hopefully, there are less than 6) that connect you to that hiring manager. Find those links and you will find yourself at the front of the line for job offers!

How name dropping led to Gary Dell'Abate's dream job.

You may not think that a man nicknamed BaBa Booey by his boss, because of a mistake he made, is at the perfect job! However, Gary Dell'Abate realized what his perfect job would look like the day he walked by a college radio studio. Dell'Abate's book "They Call Me Baba Booey" details his career from college internships all the way to his celebrity status as executive producer of the Howard Stern Show, a job that he absolutely loves.

Dell'Abate wrote that getting started in the radio industry was extremely difficult for him, but it was a link between him, an old boss, and a stranger at NBC, that helped him win the job offer that would change his life.

Before arriving for a job interview at NBC, Dell'Abate had spoken to his old boss Steve North about the position. North mentioned that he had a friend named Nell at the station and that if he ran into her, he should say "Steve says hi". As it happened Dell'Abate did overhear a woman in the elevator call her companion "Nell".

Dell'Abate then approached her and asked if she was the same Nell, Steve's friend. This introduction led Nell, a senior manager at the station, to personally escort Dell'Abate to his interview and tell the hiring manager, "If Steve North recommends him he must be good." Dell'Abate got the job at NBC, and would eventually meet Howard Stern and become his executive producer.

Who is the decision maker?

Your job is to get your resume and solution in front of the decision maker rather than the various levels of gatekeepers waiting to intercept your application. Find out who the decision maker is by researching the company. Just like you want to be familiar with the company, you want to be familiar with who the decision maker is. Your research should also help you find the most direct method of contacting the decision maker.

Meeting with decision makers.

When you meet with the decision maker be prepared with something you have in common. Bob was a salesman, but wasn't applying for a sales position. That didn't stop him from using one of his tried and true sales secrets when he entered the office of the decision maker for his job interview.

He took several seconds to scan the details of the office. He was looking for something that he had in common with the decision maker. He noticed an autographed Mario Lemieux picture on a shelf. He had just noticed Lemieux on a flight from Pittsburgh and Lemieux had posed for a picture with him. Bob mentioned the picture and then his flight. The interviewer was excited to spend a few minutes talking about hockey and his fond Lemieux memories. The decision maker had a good feeling about Bob as he started the interview.

Do you need a new email address?

Take this quick test. Read these email addresses and assess the first thing that comes to your mind. HotAngel21@xyz.com, partydawg1@abc.net, and krazykilla@asd.com.

Now read AngelaThorton21@xyz.com, PeteDawson@abyz.net, and KerryKilmer@asd.com. See a difference?

Now imagine what a hiring manager will think. Just like the clothes you wear, the tattoos you expose, and the words you say, your email address sends a particular message about you and your personality. What would you like a hiring manager to think?

Interviewing Behind Enemy Lines

One of the best sources of a new job is your former employer's competition. Everyone has a competitor, but believe it or not, the competitor is not always in as bad a position as the company that laid you off. They may actually be looking to expand and hire. It isn't uncommon for a company to interview and hire many of their competitors laid off workers.

Why wouldn't they? If the two (or more) companies are similar, a company may find a very good match for their business versus hiring someone with little or no industry experience. Any company would be glad to snag their competitor's best talent, thus strengthening and reinforcing their own position within the industry.

As an industry insider you may already know who the key players are over at the competition's headquarters. Give them a call. What do you have to lose? The worst that can happen is that they are also struggling and can't hire right now. The best that could happen is that they are excited to get their hands on one of the key assets (YOU) of their competitor and make you a job offer equivalent or better than what you previously had.

There is one potential setback to this strategy that you should be aware of. In the frenzied excitement of watching Company A falter, Company B decides to get cheap. This is particularly true when Company A is going out of business permanently and Company B knows you have no chance of being recalled back to work.

In this case they are interested enough to hire you and add your expertise to their company, but they make you a salary offer that is substantially less than what you were making, explaining that you are brand new to them and that their pay rates certainly weren't anywhere close to the "ridiculous" amounts Company A was paying.

What should you do in this case? Take the job. You will most likely be far better off working there than you would be collecting unemployment insurance payments. However, don't hesitate to drop this job if you have the opportunity to work elsewhere at your old rate or better.

Interview Behaviors Employers Can't Resist

Let's see your teeth.

In the 2007 documentary "Skid Row", Pras Michel (of hip-hop group The Fugees) lived undercover as a homeless person for over a week in order to better understand their plight. During that time, he had to find money in order to buy food. When he first arrived at skid row he went from car to car begging for quarters.

At the end of his first day he noted that when he smiled at the people he was asking for spare change he received a lot more. Michel said, "I am not the type of dude that likes to smile. Hustling up there, man let me tell you something, people pay me to smile. From this point on, I am always going to smile, man!"

A pleasant smile is inviting and elicits trust from others. Considering that most people make a judgment about you within a few seconds of meeting, a smile will help ensure a hiring manager views you in a positive light.

Would you like an interviewer to see you as confident and smile back at you? Here are a couple of interesting facts about smiling from pickthebrain.com:

1) Smiling helps you get promoted: Smiles make a person seem more attractive, sociable and confident, and people who smile more are more likely to get a promotion.

2) Smiles are contagious: It's not just a saying: smiling really is contagious, scientists say. In a study conducted in Sweden, people had difficulty frowning when they looked at other subjects who were smiling, and their muscles twitched into smiles all on their own.

Another interesting insight about smiling was mentioned in the February 26, 2011 Business Insider article "If You Look Like This, Your Pay Check Will Be Higher Than Average", which references many studies on physical appearance and the likelihood of being hired or promoted. One study mentioned "subjects ranked people who were smiling as more trustworthy than people with straight faces."

How would you like to immediately be considered more of the following:

-Attractive
-Popular with the opposite sex
-A success in your career
-Intelligent
-Happy
-Friendly
-Interesting
-Kind
-Sensitive to other people

Well according to Beall Research and Training of Chicago all it takes to appear more attractive, intelligent, interesting, successful and wealthy is white, healthy looking teeth!

528 people were divided into two groups. Both groups viewed pictures of the same 8 people. The pictures of people were exactly the same except for one difference: their teeth. Half of the

528 people viewed pictures before minor cosmetic dentistry, the other half viewed pictures of the same people, but now they had straight, white teeth. The group who viewed the pictures of people with white, healthy looking teeth, as the only difference, ranked each of the 8 people in the pictures higher in the 10 categories you see above!

A waggin' tail greeting.

If you are a dog owner you know what it is like to come home and have your pet at the door wagging his tail in excitement. Doesn't it feel good when someone is that happy to see you? Your dog isn't just standing there to welcome you, he is obviously ecstatic you are back!

You don't have a tail to wag, but the greeting you give to anyone who has a part in interviewing, testing, assessing, or hiring you should look pretty close that the one your dog gives you. Enthusiasm is contagious, and you want these people to be enthusiastic about you.

Do the obvious things. Stand up. Extend your hand. Greet everyone. Thank everyone. Give everyone a large smile. Make eye contact. Show energy and enthusiasm. You will be the only person that does this and it will be one more reason you move to the front of the line. Now, for goodness sake, don't lick the interviewer's face!

Having something (or someone) in common is more important than references.

It is no secret that people tend to like people that have common interests or traits such as their own. Some psychologists suggest that this tendency is written into our genes and it is just the course of nature. Other experts say that is only half the story; that environmental factors also play a role in our choices of favorite people. Those people have something in common with you. Two people may prefer each other's company because they both love baseball, for example.

The interview process is very much a relationship building exercise. You have precious few minutes in order to get and then keep the busy interviewer's attention. Obviously one of the fastest ways to keep her attention is to have something in common.

How do you know what you both have in common? What if you have nothing in common with the interviewer? First of all it would be hard to believe you can't identify one thing you have in common with the interviewer, considering you are both seated in an office at XYZ Company. At this moment you have XYZ Company in common. However, let's pretend you are at a complete loss and have nothing in common. In this case you can fake it or be the most interested person the interviewer has ever met.

You do love covered bridges, right?

The interviewer loves covered bridges. She has pictures of covered bridges in her office. She has a model of a covered bridge in her office. Her stationary has covered bridges on it. For the life of you, you can't see the appeal of a covered bridge. However, all of a sudden you are the biggest covered bridge fan. You have a question about that picture, a compliment about the stationary, and admiration at the workmanship on the model bridge.

Before you say that is deceitful, ask yourself is it so wrong to show genuine interest in someone else's passion? Secondly, ask yourself if you would like to be the person the interviewer remembers with fondness.

I always feel like somebody's watching me.

Just like there are behaviors employers love there are also behaviors that make employers cringe. In fact employers will be watching you very closely and evaluating how you conduct yourself and interact with others. That means it is very important you are aware of your own actions when interviewing.

In "The Pick" episode of Seinfeld, Jerry is unjustly dumped by his new girlfriend when she thinks she sees him picking his nose in the car beside hers. While Jerry would argue that he was only scratching, the girlfriend continued to believe it was a pick based on the angle from which she saw Jerry. Have you ever been in a situation where a seemingly innocent act is completely misunderstood? One place you certainly don't want this to happen is at a potential employer's workplace.

Keep in mind that as you are pulling into the parking lot of the company you are interviewing at, you are being watched. Nearly every company has a security camera or at least a bored employee gazing out a window. As the new guy every one of your actions, no matter how small, is being judged.

Spitting on the sidewalk at your job interview.

Did you take the premium parking spot? Did you throw a cigarette butt on the ground? Were you speeding? Remember that you are being watched and evaluated from the moment you arrive at your job interview. Don't let your guard down; behave as if you are being interviewed even as you walk toward the building.

In the "Ron and Marie" episode of *Breakthroughs with Tony Robbins* on NBC, Ron was given the opportunity to start a new career at Uncle Jack's Steakhouse and earn a salary of $100,000.00.

On his very first day as a manager trainee Ron was outside making sure the restaurant was clean when the manager spotted him spitting on the sidewalk in front of the restaurant. The manager immediately walked up to Ron and fired him, stating that type of behavior was disrespectful to the restaurant and customers. Don't let something like that happen to you!

Zap The Dreaded Employment Gap

One of the standard questions you will find on preprinted interview forms is a request to explain any gaps in your employment history. You may think that question is asked in order to find out if you like to take long periods of leisure time off from work, but there is a somewhat valid reason why employers ask that question.

It is the same unfortunate reason some employers shy away from hiring people who are unemployed. The concern is that the longer you've been away from a job, there is a greater tendency for you to lose basic, but essential, work skills.

This means skills such as working as part of team, reporting to a supervisor, adhering to a schedule, following a dress code, and maintaining a positive attitude. One way to counteract this opinion is being involved and working on something that you can put on your resume. Just about anything would be better than nothing as long as it shows some kind of responsible action would have been taken by you on a consistent basis.

The best defense against an employer hung up on employment gaps is to not show any employment gaps. Fill the gap with some productive task that can be related to work. You've had a part-time job, you've been attending college classes in order to complete your degree, you've been speaking at civic organizations on topics from your industry, or you've been working (actually volunteering, but say "working") at some charitable organization performing your regular work skills.

Why part-time work?

A part-time job during times of unemployment or underemployment serves you in several ways. A part-time job eliminates the job gap on your resume. In 2011 an unfortunate trend of companies bypassing otherwise qualified job candidates because of an employment gap was taking hold.

The February 17, 2011 Yahoo! News article "Help Wanted - jobless need not apply" stated "Job-placement professionals say that over the last year, more and more employers have made it clear they won't consider job candidates who aren't working." "Some employers have said they're unwilling to hire unemployed workers because they believe that if a worker has once been let go, that's a sign that he or she is probably not a great hire."

Even Federal Reserve Chair Ben Bernanke was quoted as saying, "...when people are out of work for a long time, their skills can erode, which may understandably make them less attractive to employers." Whether you are working 15 hours or 55 hours a week you will still have a current job to list on your resume. This form of discrimination is wrong, but not currently illegal, so you must prepare for this reality during your job search. Eliminating the employment gap question is just one benefit of a part-time job.

Earlier in this chapter we discussed ways to reduce expenses. Why not take a part-time job with an employer who offers generous employee discounts? Part-time employees at the furniture retailer I worked for received a discount on furniture. Their discount was "cost plus 10%" which typically meant a true 50% off the price customers were paying.

A part-time position can also give you the opportunity for paid training while enhancing or learning marketable job skills. Choose a part-time job that is going to teach you something you can leverage into a higher paid full-time position. Consider the example Henry Ford gave.

Henry Ford's part-time job.

In his mid-20s Henry Ford was still an employee for someone else, but he found many ways to get better with machinery and tools in his "off the clock" time. He took a part time job with a jeweler, and using the skill of watch repair he learned on the job, he became much better with mechanical parts by repairing hundreds of watches. That newly honed skill, of course, led to his ability to build cars and ultimately an extremely successful business.

Remember the partial unemployment compensation benefit!

While receiving unemployment compensation you will be allowed, and encouraged, to work. In fact you will receive a notice that discusses the "partial unemployment compensation benefit". As discussed in Chapter 3, this means you can earn up to a particular amount of money and still collect your entire unemployment benefit. Example: based on your previous full-time earnings and work history you may be eligible for a $250.00 per week unemployment payment, but you may also earn $125.00 without a reduction in the $250.00 you are already getting. $375.00 coming into the household each week is much nicer than $250.00!

ASK For The Job!

Do you know what the number one way to close a sale is? ASK for the sale! The same is true with your job interview. Now that you have reached the end of the interview you MUST ask for a commitment on the interviewer's part. Very few applicants will do this.

Too many job seekers don't specifically ask for the job for the same reason some salespeople don't ask for the sale. They are afraid of rejection. Even professional salespeople know you are not going to close every sale. So do not be disappointed if your request to be hired is ignored, refused, or rejected.

Your job interview is just like a sales call, and many of the same strategies that work during the selling process apply to job interviewing. A salesperson identifies the customer's need and works to find a solution. You should do the same thing at your interview. Research the company. Find out what their problems and opportunities are. Bring those up in your interview and talk about solutions you can provide if hired.

Sales people are sure to leave something in their prospect's hands. You should do the same both before and after the interview. Give the hiring manager another copy of your resume prior to the interview. This shows that you come to meetings prepared. After the interview give the manager a list of the top 10 reasons to hire you, or a written suggestion on how to solve the company's problem.

Work From Home

Anyone from western Pennsylvania will remember the winter storms from February 2010 and again in February 2011. In fact the 2011 winter storms affected states all across the country. The incredible amount of snow and ice shut down roads, closed schools, stopped businesses from opening their doors, and caused a tremendous amount of home and property damage. Were you in a position where you had to drive to work through all of that? If so, did you ever wish you could give up the commute (snow or no snow) and just work from home?

There are many reasons to work from home today. Consider the financial and time cost of commuting, for example. There are also fuel, insurance, and car maintenance costs. The average commute time is about 24 minutes one way; almost 1 hour every day. What else could you be doing with an extra hour each day?

Examples of work at home jobs you can find.

The Tribune Review newspaper in Pittsburgh ran an article in early 2010 that pointed out there are many types of work you can do from home. For example, you can work as a customer support representative, sales person, or virtual concierge from your home office. A few other examples are freelance work such as graphic design, data entry, taking surveys, and mystery shopping via the phone and internet.

One problem people run into when looking for work at home positions is finding credible companies to work for. When you search online for work at home opportunities you will often find people offering to help you for a fee. These are not legitimate options.

Companies that hire work at home employees.

Alpine Access is an example of an organization that offers work at home jobs. Alpine Access provides customer service to many organizations that need to supplement their own workforce or are not in a position to create their own customer service department. Alpine Access agents work from home and answer calls from customers of Alpine's clients. Examples of other organizations that do this are LiveOps.com and WorkingSolutions.com.

Many national companies, such as 1-800-FLOWERS and 1-800-CONTACTS, will also occasionally hire work at home agents through their own programs. A great resource to find these jobs is WorkAtHomeDesk.com. If you ever wanted to work with a specific company, but they did not have local job openings, or were not close enough to your home, the work from home option may provide you a way to get your foot in the door.

Are you finding jobs close to home?

Remember, that you do have to meet the criteria of the work at home employer. Having high speed internet access, appropriate office equipment, and the technical ability to use that equipment are always basic requirements.

Finally, a reason to explore work from home options is your local economy. Working from home allows you to apply for jobs across the country, not just in your own locality. You can find part-time or full-time work in a variety of industries. If you find yourself in a position where you can't leave your home or you are finding few local job opportunities, take a look at working from home.

Peace Corps

The Peace Corps may be another option for the right person who isn't finding meaningful work here in the United States. The Peace Corps offers many benefits and opportunities in trade you're your commitment of time. Involvement with the Peace Corps means paid full-time work and an opportunity to build others up with your education and work expertise.

The Peace Corps is always hiring! 4,000 volunteers are needed every year to replace those who are returning from their service countries. However, the Peace Corps doesn't just bring anyone on. They are looking for the right people for the type of work they help others with.

Areas that the Peace Corp provides assistance to other countries include:

-Education   -Health and HIV/AIDS

-Agriculture   -Environment

-Business and Information Technology

-Youth and Community Development

Are you right for the Peace Corps?

The Peace Corps says a successful volunteer would possess the following traits:

-Self-reliance   -Sense of humor

-Patience   -Relevant work skills

-Responsible   -Adaptable

-Flexible   -Positive

Additionally, you are required to make a 27 month long commitment to the Peace Corps. Applicants to the Peace Corps must be at least 18 years old. You must be free from legal entanglements and physically capable for performing the work you will be assigned, thus you must pass their medical qualification testing. Having a bachelor's degree is very helpful in that 90% of the positions within the Peace Corps require a bachelor's degree.

Tangible benefits of volunteering with the Peace Corps.

Even though the people that participate within the Peace Corps are referred to as volunteers, there are several economic benefits given to them. Here are some of them.

Pay and Living Expenses

Volunteers receive an allowance that will allow them to live in a manner similar to the people among whom they will work and reside with.

Transportation

The cost of transportation to and from the country of service is paid for.

Medical and Dental Care

Medical and dental care is provided at no charge by the Peace Corps.

Language Training

Volunteers must learn a foreign language. That training is part of the 27 month commitment and is paid for.

Readjustment Allowance

A readjustment allowance of $7,425.00 is given to volunteers upon the completion of their commitment in order to help them readjust to life in the States.

Vacation Days

Volunteers receive 2 vacation days per month and may use them however they please. Travel during a vacation day is at the volunteer's own expense.

Cancellation of Perkins Student Loans

Volunteers with Perkins Student Loans may be eligible to receive a partial cancellation of their loan.

Intangible benefits you may receive.

If you want to really put your work expertise to the test, you'll find that opportunity with the Peace Corps. Teaching others how to do what you do is one of the best ways to hone your own skills. Additionally, the work you do is an excellent resume builder. Few people will hold the same experience you do once you've spent time volunteering with the Peace Corps.

Finally, helping others better themselves through the structured approach found in the Peace Corps is good for your spirit. Watching others thrive because of your investment in them will be emotionally rewarding. You can learn more about the Peace Corps at peacecorps.gov.

Chapter 6

Resources

Chapter Overview

In this chapter you will find a quick review of the variety of many of the resources and ideas discussed throughout this book. You will also discover additional resources that can help stretch your money and preserve the standard of living you are accustomed to. Some of these ideas will help you financially during periods of unemployment, while others can serve you at any time.

Resources

Your County Health Department

An example of a county's health department resources for the under/unemployed is "Allegheny County's Guide To Health Care Resources" found online. It is a comprehensive resource for information on low or no cost medical, dental, vision, and preventative care, as well as, health clinics, smoking cessation programs, and WIC (the Woman, Infants, and Children program).

COBRA Coverage

The Consolidated Omnibus Budget Reconciliation Act (COBRA) is a law that provides continuation of group health coverage that otherwise might be lost when you are laid off. Under COBRA you pay the full premium that the company was paying for your insurance, but you get to keep your coverage, which is especially important if you were already in need of health care. All of your rights are listed on the Department of Labor's website.

The Unemployment / CareerLink Office

The unemployment office's main task is to find you a new job and provide resources to assist you in that endeavor. Visit these professionals, explain your goals and needs, and let their experts give you an orientation through the many resources they provide.

The Library

There are many reasons to make the public library your new office once unemployed. The library is a wealth of resources providing such items as: computers, a variety of software, internet access, tax help, copying and printing service, job search assistance, educational classes, a quiet meeting place, and much, much more.

The Community College

As mentioned in Chapter 4 many community colleges offer tuition waivers for unemployed workers. Visit your community college's admission office, explain your situation, and ask for information on all programs offered to assist you in updating your education and finding work.

The College Financial Aid Office

The amount of tuition money you qualify for through your state may not cover all of your retraining expenses. Visit your chosen school's financial aid office and ask for their expertise in your particular situation.

Your Former Bosses

Because of the nature of their jobs, many of your ex-bosses may have larger professional networks than you do. Don't hesitate to reconnect with them, join their network, and meet the hiring managers they connect with.

Former Human Resources Staff and Recruiters

Perhaps even more so than your former boss, these professionals are well connected in the business community. They actively network with other recruiting pros so that they can share leads on qualified applicants. Tap into their network and be sure they know what your qualifications are.

The Internet

Access to a web connection is a must while unemployed. You will need specific answers and information that allows you to avoid costly mistakes and wasted time. The web will provide you access to the expertise you need during this trying time. Can't afford web access? Try the library or a Wi-Fi hotspot.

Temp Agencies

Temporary agency managers are some of the most connected people you will meet. Their entire day is spent reaching out to employers and finding jobs. Need a full or part-time job right away? Talk to these job finding pros.

CHIP Program

The Children's Health Insurance Program is a nationwide program, overseen individually by each state; it provides subsidized health insurance for all children.

How much the parents make is one factor in determining if the coverage will be free or low cost, and in Pennsylvania all children are eligible for this program, regardless of their parents' income. The eligibility chart for Pennsylvania residents can be found at http://www.chipcoverspakids.com/assets/media/pdf/2009_income_guidelines.pdf.

The Auctioneer

On one hand you may find a live auction to be a cheap form of entertainment. It can be exciting to listen to a professional and entertaining auctioneer, and watch people bid against each other.

On the other hand you may be simply interested in the incredible deals you can find at auctions. Use auctionzip.com to find items at auction close to you. Use auctions to buy just about anything you may *need* to buy or replace. You will often find those same items for 90% less than you would in a store.

Job Fairs

As mentioned before, job fairs are a great place to find and interview with many employers all at once. In Pittsburgh you can use TheQuarterRoll.com to find local job fair listings. Another resource is The Employment Guide's website, which offers a tool for finding local job fairs across the country. You can find it at http://pittsburgh.employmentguide.com/.

LIHEAP

The Low Income Home Energy Assistance Program is a federally funded program that provides grant money to those in need. The following chart was effective as of July 2011 and details the income limits for those requesting assistance.

Household Size	Monthly Income	Annual Income
1	$1,444	$17,328
2	$1,943	$23,312
3	$2,441	$29,296
4	$2,940	$35,280
5	$3,439	$41,264
6	$3,937	$47,248
7	$4,436	$53,232
8	$4,935	$59,216

For each additional household member add $5,984.00 per year

Medicine

If you are faced with losing your prescription coverage or will struggle to pay for medicine, consider alternative sources for free or low cost prescriptions. Your doctor's office would likely be able to recommend sources of free medicine.

Many pharmacies offer no or low cost generic medicine. Giant Eagle grocery store advertises free antibiotics and 90 days supplies of over 400 generic medications for $10.00 each. Additionally, many pharmaceutical companies offer programs to supply free medicine to those who are unemployed and in need. Pfizer's "Maintain" program is one such example.

SNAP Program

The Supplemental Nutrition Assistance Program (SNAP) is the name for the federal Food Stamp Program. The following chart will show what the income limits are for those applying for aid.

Household Size	Gross monthly income (130% of poverty)	Net monthly income (100% of poverty)
1	$1,174	$903
2	1,579	1,215
3	1,984	1,526
4	2,389	1,838
5	2,794	2,150
6	3,200	2,461

| 7 | 3,605 | 2,773 |
| 8 | 4,010 | 3,085 |

Dress For Success

Dressing appropriately for job interviews is one key in getting the employment offer. However, it may have been a long time since your needed clothes for an interview or new job environment.

Charities such as Dress For Success in Pittsburgh, Pennsylvania, offer assistance to women in need of professional clothing for a new job, but are struggling with the financial cost of new clothing. Other organizations such as the Salvation Army and Goodwill can help as well.

Free GED Classes

It is a fact that people who have dropped out of high school will face a serious disadvantage in finding meaningful work. Combine that with a struggling economy and companies reluctant to hire and you are in for a tough uphill battle.

Obtaining a General Equivalency Diploma can make getting hired much easier and there are many programs available to allow you to do that for free. The unemployment office and the local community college are two great resources for getting more information.

Loss History Reports

Also known as C.L.U.E. reports (Comprehensive Loss Underwriting Exchange) these reports are provided to insurers so that they can evaluate your past insurance claims. These reports become part of an insurer's own formula for determining your insurability and how much you are going to pay.

Just like with credit reports, you obviously would want to insure that the information on an insurance loss history report is correct. Errors on your report could result in higher insurance premiums, so be sure to check your report for accuracy. The link found in "Chapter Resources" will take you to the Lexis-Nexis website where you can request free copies of your loss history report.

Second Free Credit Report

If you have already received a free credit report in the last 12 months, but are now unemployed and planning to apply for jobs in the next 60 days, you are entitled to a second free credit report. The reason for this is because many employers include your credit report as part of their hiring decision. Make sure that you know what it says before they do.

Blogger

There is a growing trend to use the Internet for interviewing purposes. One way to do that is to create a website that promotes you as a choice job candidate. Blogger is Google's free website builder that provides you with easy to use templates and tools.

Blogger's software will allow you to create a virtual resume unlike any other application or resume a hiring manager will see. Use this tool to creatively highlight your work experience, solutions, and accomplishments.

Google Docs

Google Docs is Google's free spreadsheet, presentation, and word processing software. You may not have software programs such as PowerPoint, Word, or Excel at home, but you may want to put together a resume or presentation. Free sites like Google Docs allow you to use software that is very similar to programs that costs hundreds of dollars. All you need is a free Google account to get started.

Free TV

Netflix, Hulu, and Fancast are examples of online sources that allow you to replace expensive cable for no or low cost. Of course the free resources online don't replace all cable programming, such as NFL events, but when stretching your money is critical these sites are great alternatives.

The Gym

Early mornings in the gym are like LinkedIn social groups in real life. The gym will be filled with working people getting a workout in before it is time to punch in. At the gym you'll get healthy exercise and access to friendships that will support your networking efforts.

Your Phone

Without a boss looking over your shoulder it may be tempting to freely text your friends the details of your day every few minutes. Rather, use your phone for cutting your expenses and finding jobs.

Call people like your insurance agent – tell her your situation and ask her for a number of ways to get a better rate. Call your former customers and tell them you would appreciate their help with job leads.

Benefits.gov

Benefits.gov is the federal government's primary website for providing information to citizens about benefits we may be entitled to. Benefits are broken down into categories. Visitors to the site are asked to fill out questionnaires. Based on your answers you will be led to the appropriate grants and programs available to you.

Free Legal Aid Pennsylvania

Legal help and representation can be costly. If you need legal help there are organizations that can direct you to free resources. For example, the Allegheny County Bar Association's "Modest Means Panel" in Pennsylvania refers those in need to attorneys working for a reduced fee. "To qualify for the Modest Means Panel, an individual must fall within 200% of the Federal Poverty Guidelines before taxes."

USAttorneyLegalServices.com provides an online directory and is another resource for free legal resources by state and county. Their website says, "In most cases, clients are eligible if their income falls below 125% of the federal poverty guidelines."

Working At Home

There are many reasons to work from home today. Consider the financial and time cost of commuting, for example. There is fuel, insurance, and car maintenance costs. As mentioned in chapter 5,

Workathomedesk.com is a source of legitimate employers, such as Alpine Access, who offer work at home jobs.

Your Vehicle

If you have access to reliable transportation you have the opportunity to get out of your home and start knocking on business doors, introducing yourself to company gatekeepers and decision makers in person, and placing a resume in the hands (not inbox) of hiring managers.

Your Wingman

Asking for a job interview is much like approaching someone for a date. You are approaching someone you may not know at all, but have an interest in, and have to put yourself in the uncomfortable position of possibly being rejected, maybe even publicly. However, using a "job interview wingman" can greatly improve your odds of getting the job.

The best job interview wingman is someone who works at the company already or knows the job interviewer. Your association with that person will give you the appearance of someone who is already closer to the inside than a stranger who is also applying for the job. You will also feel more confident approaching the interviewer as you already have something in common: your wingman.

Senior Citizen Property Tax Relief Program

Just because you are 60 years old doesn't mean you can't be laid off as well. If you are 60 or over, the county you live in may have a special assistance program to help reduce your property tax burden. In Allegheny County, Pennsylvania, you can find the link to help at: http://www.alleghenycounty.us/treasure/act77.aspx

Your Time

When you worked for someone else that person controlled how you spent your time. Now you have the freedom to spend your time the way you want to. However, with that freedom comes the responsibility to use your time effectively. Your time is your most valuable asset. Use it wisely. This is an opportunity to do things that will strengthen your future economic security and marketability.

Your Smile

Your smile is the second most important asset you have. It costs nothing, is fully within your control, and has a powerful ability to instantaneously win trust and confidence from others. In a time when you may think you have fewer reasons to smile you will discover that smiling opens up doors of opportunity.

Your Attitude

The most important asset you have is your attitude. You have got to believe that you will come out of unemployment better than you went into it. Believe that you have the power to make yourself better off tomorrow than you are today. Believe that you now have many options at your disposal to make yourself more marketable and attractive to employers, lower your living costs, maintain your standard of living, and effectively manage the risks to your financial position. Believe that when you apply the knowledge you now have with the hard work you will perform, you will look back and see what was actually an opportunity that led to a stronger financial position and a more satisfying career.

Make your resume unique!

ADDRESS: PITTSBURGH, PENNSYLVANIA
PHONE: 412-376-7283
ONLINE: THEQUARTERROLL.COM
EMAIL: MIKE@THEQUARTERROLL.COM

MIKE BOWMAN

EXPECTED RELEASE DATE

SEPTEMBER 2011

UNEMPLOYMENT DESK

"HOW TO SCARE THE HELL OUT OF UNEMPLOYMENT"

20 YEARS OF BUSINESS EXPERIENCE

DUQUESNE UNIVERSITY ALUMNI
Bachelors Degree - *Professional Leadership*
Executive Certificate in Financial Planning
Certified Financial Planner program

WHAT I'VE DONE

Astronaut - NASA
Houston, TX / June 2004-June 2007

Firefighter
Los Angeles, CA / June 2001-May 2004

Fighter Jet Pilot - U.S. Navy
Norfolk, VA / June 1998-May 2001

Docent - Monticello
Charlottesville, VA / June 1995-May 1998

WHAT I DO

MAGAZINE PUBLISHING
I publish The Quarter Roll Magazine. The only personal finance magazine that provides "financial entertainment".

PODCASTING
Produce podcasts from the content published online and in print form from The Quarter Roll.

BOOK WRITING
Write books on more in depth topics such as unemployment and understanding financial based behaviors.

PUBLIC SPEAKING
Present personal finance "how to" topics to businesses and individuals.

IF YOU CAUGHT ME NOT WORKING

You would find me at the gym or on an adventure with my family exploring history, museums, national parks, and forgotten national treasures.

SEE ME AT WORK
Scan Here

WHAT I KNOW

ADOBE
- INDESIGN
- ILLUSTRATOR
- PHOTOSHOP
- FLASH
- DREAMWEAVER

MICROSOFT
- WORD
- POWERPOINT
- EXCEL
- FRONT PAGE

GOOGLE
- FEEDBURNER
- ANALYTICS
- ADWORDS

WHAT I'VE LEARNED

- Simultaneously managing several projects
- Managing large groups of employees
- How to cut my grocery bill by 90%
- How to use social media to tell the world about doing better financially
- Getting $1.25 for every $1.00
- Finding fascinating, but very inexpensive adventures to go on
- Creating impactful ways of getting my message out

PRESIDENT OBAMA
1600 Pennsylvania Avenue, NW
Washington, DC 20500
(202) 456-1414

SENATOR BOEHNER
East Capitol Street
Washington, DC 20500
(202) 224-312

PA GOVERNOR CORBETT
225 Main Capitol Building
Harrisburg, Pennsylvania 17120
(717) 787-2500

WHO I KNOW

Conclusion

"There is one thing I want you to do for me. Win."
- Adrian to Rocky in Rocky 2

Unemployment is hard. It is a fight you didn't pick, but is a fight you must win. Unemployment has the potential to hurt you permanently. In this book's introduction we discussed economic scarring. That means unemployment will whittle away at your assets, and that can include your savings, home equity, and even your health. The longer you go without a reasonable amount of income the more those things will decay.

This means you will be in an economically weakened state, and less able to combat the financial challenges that Life is notorious for throwing at any one of us, always at the worst times. People will always get sick or hurt, cars/appliances/stuff will always break down, and you will still want to be warm and fed, regardless of how much utility rates and food prices go up.

Underemployment and unemployment won't just hurt you today. Every day your income is reduced by 10%/50%/80% your future well-being is being threatened. As you dip into savings, give up routine health care, stop changing your car's oil, or cancel insurance policies because you have less money today, you are potentially setting yourself up for bigger problems tomorrow.

That is when unemployment comes in for the knockout punch. That is how you get permanently scarred economically. In this book we've seen a number of ways to delay that affect. Your ability to earn a good living, however, still remains the absolute best way to preserve and advance your standard of living.

Just like a professional fighter, unemployment doesn't just wear you down physically, it wears you down mentally. It preys on the mind games you play with yourself when you begin to doubt your self-worth and wonder what you did wrong. You've got to remember, it doesn't matter if you did or didn't do something wrong. You can set that debate aside for another day.

The fact is, that like millions of other people, your livelihood is being imminently threatened and that is what you must focus all of your physical and mental energy on resolving. Your primary goal is apply the knowledge you have gained through years of work, from this book, and the other resources available to you and win back your quality of life.

Triple H's story

On May 21, 2009 during a professional wrestling match, Paul Michael Lévesque, also known in the ring as Triple H, tore a portion of his quadriceps muscle off of his leg bone. An injury of this magnitude can easily end an athlete's career, but Triple H was determined to get back on his feet, and back to work, as quickly as possible.

After his surgery he aggressively exercised through the intense physical therapy that was required to heal his leg. Always known for his work ethic, Triple H was applauded by doctors for working extraordinarily hard at getting back to his job. At that moment in time, Triple H considered rehabilitation as his full-time job; a task that would allow him to get back to the ring as quickly as possible. That meant he would have to work even harder than he was already famously known for.

Being away from his job was not easy for Triple H. There were times he felt lonely and disconnected. He quickly realized that work was a huge part of his life. Motivated to get back more quickly, he set small goals for himself every day that would push him forward in his rehabilitation.

His rehabilitation specialist, Dr. Andrews, stated Triple H's motivation was higher than any patient he had ever worked with. The specialist would ask Triple H to do 10 repetitions of an exercise and he would do 20.

Triple H said, "When I got injured and they told me how bad it was after my surgery I never thought of anything else other than 'Well, looks like I am not leaving Birmingham until this is better'. I'll move here, I'll live in this hotel, I'll come to rehab at 9 in the morning when the place opens and I will be there until 6 at night when the place closes and I will do everything I can possibly do to this leg to get it better."

At the end of 8 months, much sooner than expected, Triple H returned to work and quickly regained the momentum he had established prior to the traumatic injury.

Commenting on the crowd's reaction to Triple H's return, Jim Ross, a longtime ring announcer for World Wrestling Entertainment said, "I've been to a lot of loud ballgames, and WWE events, all the way back to the 70s from doing wrestling and I don't know if I've ever heard an ovation, just an animalistic gutter roll, a 'we really feel for ya, we want you back, we're embracing you'. It's got to be one of Triple H's most memorable nights and in his life. Not just in his career, but his life."

You may not experience physical pain in your job loss; however, just like Triple H worked intensely through his challenges to get back to work, you must also work extraordinarily hard to get back on your feet. Your first day back to work may not be as loud as

Triple H's with 20,000 people celebrating your success, but you will certainly feel like it. Think about that day in your mind and use it to motivate yourself to higher levels of effort in getting back to work. How will you apply this level of intensity to your own personal situation? Consider how Maureen Smith did it.

Maureen Smith's story

Apollo: "You're going down." Rocky "No. No way."
- The 15th round, Rocky 2

September 11, 2001 touched all of our lives in a variety of ways. For Maureen Smith it was the resulting slowdown of the economy that directly affected her family. Until that event Maureen had been working as a self-employed house cleaner. She had several clients that paid her well.

Unfortunately, luxuries such as having your home cleaned were one of the first things people gave up when their income shrank. It didn't take long before Maureen was no longer self-employed, but rather unemployed. Her income reduction was creating a dire problem. Even when she was working every day, Maureen's income was just enough to help the family make ends meet. Now, her family's well-being was being directly threatened, and she had no intention of accepting that.

For the longest time Maureen had been a stay at home mom. She had various entry level jobs throughout her adult life, but many years were simply spent at home raising her 3 children. She knew she had to find a job, but had few work skills that stood out on a resume.

Not deterred, and fueled by the need to provide for her family, she took stock of the skills she did have. Maureen was energetic, personable, witty, and very hard working. She was very comfortable interacting with just about any personality, and was obviously not afraid to get her hands dirty, whether literally or figuratively!

She poured her energy into finding work. Looking for work was her work! She found a job for a customer service representative in a call center; a job she had no direct experience doing. This job sounded perfect, however. It paid almost as much as she was making cleaning houses, was just minutes away from her home, and the night shift would allow her to still clean houses during the day as customers came back.

Maureen was determined to get this job. She created both a paper resume and an online resume. Using a blogging website she posted her resume online. She reasoned that because the company stressed familiarity with the internet this would be viewed favorably and perhaps calm any concerns about her lack of experience. She also eliminated an employment gap on her resume. While she hadn't been working full time for a few years, she did occasionally help her brother sell baseball cards at weekend sports shows. She listed that job during the years she worked at the shows.

Next, she got a wingman. In the course of researching the company, she discovered a news article about the company's president. He had been at a car show displaying an antique car. Maureen asked her husband, also an antique car fan, if anyone in his car club knew this president.

Her husband made a call to the club director and sure enough he knew the president. The club director then sent an email to the company president saying he had met Maureen before, she had an interview scheduled at the company that week, and thought she would make a good representative. While this certainly didn't guarantee any preferential treatment, Maureen knew it couldn't hurt!

During the interview Maureen came out strong. She had done her homework and was well aware of the challenges and successes this company was having. Maureen highlighted her ability to use the web and stressed that while she hadn't worked in a call center before she was quite comfortable working with the public as demonstrated in her past jobs.

She smiled often during the interview and was quick to develop a rapport with the hiring manager. As she was given a tour of the facility she greeted both employees and customers as if she was already working there!

At the end of the interview, Maureen asked for the job. She wasn't going to wait for a job offer. The hiring manager smiled and said no one else had directly asked for the job! Her personality, preparation, and persistence won her a job offer!

The story didn't end there, however. Yes, Maureen had been out of work for three weeks, and now she had a new job. Things had changed though. Maureen had looked unemployment in the eyes and realized how vulnerable she and her family had been. She was grateful for this entry level job, and realized that it could have been much worse. She also realized that nothing guaranteed this wouldn't happen again. She needed to prepare for the future.

Maureen used this new job not only as a means of bringing enough income home to pay the bills, but as an opportunity to advance herself professionally. Even though she had no college education or highly marketable work experience, she had a strong work ethic, the ability to solve problems others shied away from, and a magnetic personality that customers and peers loved.

Maureen knew that just like a school yard bully shies away from the kid who will stand up to him, unemployment seems to think twice before going after a person who is highly desirable in the marketplace and capable of creating other income options. Keeping her eye on strengthening her economic security, Maureen leveraged the skills she did have into new job opportunities at the same company, promotions, and raises.

In the following years she worked for two more call centers. With each move, she accepted higher level positions and pay. While most people are content with their usual 2-4% annual pay increase, Maureen had increased her pay by nearly 300% in the 8 years since her unemployment.

Not one to slip into a cocoon of comfort and forget that unemployment lurks around many corners, Maureen started her own part-time travel business. "Just in case" something were to ever happen to the terrific job she now had, she was creating her own Plan B. Maureen had not only beaten unemployment, but completely destroyed it in her life.

Scaring the hell out of unemployment

"Yo Adrian! I did it!" - Rocky to Adrian in Rocky 2

In a sense unemployment scares success into many people. Just as we saw in the examples of Triple H and Maureen, they not only get back to work, but far surpass their previous level of income and career success. This book wasn't about *us* being scared, though.

You can accomplish your employment goal and come back stronger than before. However, as we've discussed, it is going to take a lot of focused work at an intensity level you may not have been accustomed to.

You know that the people who will end up worse off from unemployment are those who won't take strategic, aggressive actions in standing up against the challenges unemployment will throw at them. They will back down and hope the bully just goes away. Not you. You know what you need to do and how to do it, now go scare the hell out of unemployment.

Chapter References

Introduction

http://www.epi.org/publications/entry/bp243/

http://www.usatoday.com/money/economy/2010-01-06-recession-scars-will-take-long-time-to-heal_N.htm

http://finance.yahoo.com/news/Signs-Youre-About-to-Get-usnews-2142260577.html?x=0&.v=1

Chapter 1

http://www.bizjournals.com/pittsburgh/print-edition/2010/12/17/job-seeker-success-pgh-workers-land-jobs.html

http://www.portal.state.pa.us/portal/server.pt?open=514&objID=552121&mode=2

http://www.suntimes.com/business/3159487-418/workers-employers-job-percent-stroud.html

http://en.thinkexist.com/

http://www.nps.gov/abli/index.htm

Chapter 2

https://www.annualcreditreport.com/cra/index.jsp

http://www.clarkhoward.com/news/personal-finance-credit/free-credit-report-info/nFbJ/

http://en.wikipedia.org/wiki/Taking_Woodstock

http://www.news-medical.net/news/20091118/Monetary-gain-and-risky-tactics-stimulate-brain-activity-says-new-study.aspx

Chapter 3

http://www.wtae.com/money/26167199/detail.html

http://www.wset.com/Global/story.asp?S=13950103

http://www.uc.pa.gov/portal/server.pt/community/uc_pa_gov/11449

http://www.calculatedriskblog.com/2010/12/tax-negotiations-no-help-for-99ers.html

http://www.nelp.org/sites/unemployedworkers/index.php/resources/resource_entry/extended_benefits

http://www.thequarterroll.com/Blog/2011/January-2011/12BetterDays.pdf

http://www.couponmom.com/

http://www.magicjack.com/6/index.asp

http://www.portal.state.pa.us/portal/server.pt?open=514&objID=599970&mode=2#sed

Chapter 4

http://www.bls.gov/news.release/empsit.t04.htm

http://www.irs.gov/newsroom/article/0,,id=210523,00.html

http://www.thepellgrant.com/

http://www.pheaa.org/stategrants/faqs.shtml#awards

http://www.mhec.state.md.us/financialaid/ProgramDescriptions/prog_fire.asp

http://benefits.infonet.upmc.com/Documents/TuitionAssistanceStaff.pdf

http://usmilitary.about.com/od/joiningthemilitary/a/enlage.htm

http://www.military.com/ASVAB

http://www.gibill.va.gov/documents/Montgomery_GI_Bill_Selected_Reserve_%28MGIB_SR_Chapter_1606%29_2010.pdf
http://www.cpms.osd.mil/ASSETS/F75D36FEF66848C5A88AF856E04007BF/user ra_faqs.pdf

http://www.celebdirtylaundry.com/2011/matt-damon-is-a-liar/

http://www.ccac.edu/default.aspx?id=151465

http://www.pittsburghlive.com/x/pittsburghtrib/news/westmoreland/s_609897.html

http://www.nvfc.org/files/documents/Volunteer_Training_White_Paper.pdf

http://www.thequarterroll.com/Blog/December-2010/unemployment-rate-unskilled-labor.htm

http://www.irs.gov/businesses/small/article/0,,id=102767,00.html

http://www.dos.state.pa.us/corps/cwp/view.asp?a=1093&q=431168.

http://www.pa100.state.pa.us/

http://www.state.pa.us/portal/server.pt/community/publications/10311

http://members.thechamberinc.com/member/newmemberapp/

http://www.careerlinkpittsburgh.com/events/index.cfm

http://www.azcentral.com/ent/celeb/articles/2011/06/07/20110607kelly-osbourne-loves-gym-helps-lift-her-mood.html

Chapter 5

http://www.imdb.com/title/tt0795381/

http://www.nbc.com/breakthrough-with-tony-robbins/

http://www.imdb.com/title/tt0697752/

http://money.cnn.com/galleries/2010/moneymag/1002/gallery.Website_donts.moneymag/2.html

Bait and Switch, Barbara Ehrenreich, 2005

http://www.businessinsider.com/if-you-have-any-of-these-20-physical-features-your-pay-check-will-probably-be-higher-2011-2#

http://pittsburgh.employmentguide.com/

http://www.thequarterroll.com/Blog/2011/April-2011/10-reasons-to-whiten-teeth.htm

http://hirejohnwilliams.com/

http://mashable.com/2011/06/16/creative-resume-designs/

Chapter 6

http://www.chipcoverspakids.com/assets/media/pdf/2009_income_guidelines.pdf

http://www.thequarterroll.com/Blog/December-2010/work-at-home.htm

http://pfizerhelpfulanswers.com/pages/Find/FindAll.aspx

http://www.usattorneylegalservices.com/free-legal-aid-Pennsylvania.html

http://www.dressforsuccesspgh.org/what-we-do/mission

http://www.alleghenycounty.us/treasure/act77.aspx

http://www.dol.gov/ebsa/faqs/faq_consumer_cobra.HTML

http://www.achd.net/chrond/pubs/pdf/Insuredlinked.pdf

http://www.acf.hhs.gov/programs/ocs/liheap/

http://www.fns.usda.gov/fns/

http://www.gianteagle.com/pharmacy/discount-generics

https://personalreports.lexisnexis.com/

http://www.blogger.com/

http://www.netflix.com/HowItWorks

http://moneysavingmom.com/store_deals/

http://www.couponsthingsbydede.com/default.asp

http://www.workathomedesk.com/directory/virtual-call-centre-jobs.htm

http://www.acbalrs.org/About/Afford-an-attorney.asp

About The Author

Mike Bowman is the owner of *The Quarter Roll* magazine, a publication about personal finance issues told through the stories of celebrities and people from various walks of life. It was the consistent worry about finances, that Mike watched too many of his peers and friends struggle with during his years in "corporate America", which led him to create *The Quarter Roll*: a better way of sharing easy-to-understand, money saving principles.

Prior to *The Quarter Roll* Mike owned other small businesses, including his company that designed and sold shooting accessories, inspired by the Colonial American era. He also worked for many years in executive management for a Top 100 furniture retailer. He received a business degree from Duquesne University in Pittsburgh, Pennsylvania, where he later returned to finish his financial planning studies.

Mike's experience running his own businesses, as well as, working as an employee for others, gives him the advantage of having worked "on both sides of the desk" as he puts it. As a business owner he sees the challenges that companies experience in creating a profit, and as a laid off employee he experienced first-hand the extreme hardships individuals face when their income is suddenly taken away.

When laid off from his long-term corporate position, Mike studied, and then taught himself and others, even more ways to get a better value for their money and to become highly marketable in the workplace. That included seeking out others who had successfully overcome unemployment and studying their success. The result of that study formed the basis for *How To Scare The Hell Out Of Unemployment*.

In his time away from work you will most likely find Mike at the gym or spending time with his family traveling across the country exploring historical locations, museums, national parks, and forgotten national treasures.